CISTERCIAN STUDIES SERIES: NUMBER SEVENTY-SIX

# THE CISTERCIAN WAY

# THE
# CISTERCIAN
# WAY

by
## André Louf

Abbot of Sainte-Marie-du-Mont
Bailleul, France

TRANSLATED BY

Nivard Kinsella
Monk of St Joseph Abbey
Roscrea, Ireland

THE CISTERCIAN MONASTERIES
OF GREAT BRITAIN AND IRELAND
1989

*First published as* La voie cistercienne: à l'école de l'amour
by Deslée de Brouwer, copyright © 1980.

First published in English as *The Cistercian Alternative* by Gill and
Macmillan Ltd., Goldenbridge, Inchicore, Dublin, Ireland, 1983.
Copyright © 1983 by the Irish Cistercian Abbots. All rights reserved.
ISBN 0 87907 976 2

Published in North America by Cistercian Publications Inc.,
WMU Station Kalamazoo, Michigan 49008, 1983.

Available in Britain and Ireland through Mount Melleray Abbey
Cappoquin, Co. Waterford, Eire.

The work of Cistercian Publications is made possible in part by
support from Western Michigan University to the
Institute of Cistercian Studies.

Designed and produced by Process Workshop Ltd, The Dairy House,
Stowell, Sherborne, Dorset.
Typeset by Electronic Village, London.
Reproduced from the Gill and Macmillan edition by Cistercian
Publications. Printed and bound in the United States of America.
Additional typesetting by Gale Akins, Kalamazoo
Photographic layout by Alice Duthie-Clark
Cover design by Linda Judy

*Cistercian Publications extends sincere appreciation to the following
communities for providing photographs of cistercian life today:*

Bolton Abbey, Moone, Co. Kildare
Caldey Abbey, Caldey Island, Dyfed
Holy Cross Abbey, Stapehill, Dorset
Mount Melleray Abbey, Cappoquin, Co. Waterford
Mount Saint Bernard Abbey, Coalville, Leicester
Mount Saint Joseph Abbey, Roscrea, Co. Tipperary
Saint Mary's Abbey, Glencairn, Co. Waterford
Sancta Maria Abbey, Nunraw, East Lothian

# Contents

ACKNOWLEDGEMENTS
The translator wishes to thank the following for permission to use copyright material.

Oxford and Cambridge University Presses for extracts from *The New English Bible*, © 1961, 1970

The Liturgical Press, Collegeville, Minnesota, for extracts from their translation of *The Rule of St Benedict*, © 1981

Cistercian Publications, Kalamazoo, Michigan, for extracts from their translations of Cisterican Fathers

Kent State University Press, Kent, Ohio, for quotations from *The Cistericans* by Louis Lekai

Dominican Publications, Dublin, for quotation from *Vatican Council II: the Conciliar and Post Conciliar Documents* edited by Austin Flannery, OP

# Introduction

The author of this book is Abbot of St Marie du Mont, or as it is commonly called, Mont-des-cats, a French monastery near the Belgian border about thirty miles from the Channel coast. In *The Cistercian Way* Dom André Louf and six of his monks who co-operated with him have presented us with a good modern statement of classic Cistercian spirituality. While the text is a joint effort involving collaboration of mind and heart, there is little doubt that it can be described as the work of a spiritual father and his disciples. For the Abbot's thought and approach are very much in evidence throughout. Dom André has a fine knowledge of the whole of monastic tradition. He has thoroughly imbibed this tradition, so that he is eminently suited for the task of producing such a work.

Deep within himself everyone has an unquenchable thirst for God—a radical need of him so that there is no ultimate rest to be found without God. This thirst for the Absolute, this dissatisfaction with what life offers, though it may appear from the outside to be central to monastic life, is not in fact at the heart of monasticism.

In baptism the Christian has had his nature transformed by grace. He enjoys the divine presence within, inviting him to personal communion. To seek to lead a deeper spiritual life, to want to lead a life of prayer, cannot be for the monk merely a greater effort to awaken and intensify that need of God which is everyone's by nature. Much more is it an opening of himself to God's grace and presence—a consent to God's call. Of its very nature Christian monasticism has to be Christ-centred, and the person who lives the monastic life is but living out his baptismal calling in a specific manner.

The kingdom of God is within the heart, and that is why St Bernard, undoubtedly the greatest of all Cistercian authors, calls on us to return to our own heart. He tells us that when we do we will find sin there, but we will also find God. Our real life has to be within the heart where God dwells. Thus the whole spiritual life turns on two hinges, as it were. These are contemplation of oneself and contemplation of God.

Contemplation of ourselves troubles us and humbles us, but out of that comes repentance which leads to salvation. Contemplation of God restores us and brings us hope and love in the Holy Spirit (see St Bernard *De Diversis* 5:1-5). Therefore without this grace-given knowledge of self there can be no monastic life. One of the great things about this book is the stress it lays on such self-knowledge. The door which opens on Paradise is within our hearts.

Since holiness is the work of grace, we simply cannot advance along this path by our own efforts. In that sense Dom André is certainly right in being wary of certain techniques and methods, especially when these come from sources which are not Christian and which therefore have a different view of man. In other sense the whole of monastic life is a method, with its traditional practices and observances. It is a way of responding to God's call in Christ and a way of preparing to be seized more and more by him.

Asceticism may now be beginning to enjoy a limited return to favour, but certainly the last few decades saw its demise. We have the outlines of a real theology of ascetisicm in this book, and a very satisfactory attempt to come to grips with the whole problem which asceticism seems to occasion for modern man. This theology is firmly rooted in the grace of the risen Christ.

If there is one exercise which is specifically monastic it is what the author prefers to call by its Latin name "*Lectio divina*" (literally, "divine reading"). Saying it is specifically monastic does not mean that those who are not monks may not engage in it, but it is something essential for the person leading the monastic life. It is no ordinary reading. It is rather a listening to, a being acted upon, a being open to the saving event of the inspired word. In the chapters dealing with it we are shown how this reading becomes prayer, and gives a unity and meaning to the whole monastic day.

While the person who feels called to the monastic life may not experience the call as strongly or as vividly as described in an early chapter of this book, the one who enters a monastery of monks or nuns will do so not only in response to a call, but also with an ideal in his or her mind. This book prepares the new arrival for the shock of discovering that the monastic life as actually lived is very different from the ideal that he or she had anticipated. But the book also encourages the person to persevere through this initial shock and to get beyond it to discover that the living reality is far richer and more diversified than he or she could ever have imagined. No house is going to provide the ideal community setting, the ideal spiritual father or mother, the ideal balance between the various elements of the life. Acceptance of real life must temper idealism. As the days go by and the newcomer settles in, he or she soon begins to grow in a love for the community and an awareness of the support the brothers or sisters provide.

Anyone who writes a book so rich in personal spiritual experience, in concrete descriptions of the monastic day, is bound to have his presentation coloured by the life as it is lived in his own community, which in turn is in a specific country. The monk or nun who has several years experience of monastic life to draw on can easily distinguish the different levels of the material presented, and recognise what is of particular and what of general application. For he or she knows what depends on local custom or circumstance and what on more universal norms. Involved here is not only the arrangement of the daily schedule and the ramifications of the local monastic economy, but something much deeper. The whole relationship of St Marie du Mont, or indeed it would seem of any other French monasteries to "the world" for example, differs considerably from what one finds in the Irish and British monasteries. The translator has coped ably with this problem, and where possible has identified these areas by a discreet use of footnotes. He is to be thanked for this and these footnotes will be of inestimable benefit to readers who do not have a monastic background.

What we are given in this book is a very positive and almost idealistic presentation of the Cistercian vocation. It is a book which will be welcomed by Cistercians all over the world, for even if it does not meet every need, or cover all the ground, there is no modern presentation of Cistercian spirituality comparable to it.

*Dom Celsus Kelly,*
*Abbot of Bethlehem Abbey,*
*Portglenone*

# Translator's Preface

Before thanking those who helped with this translation, I wish to note the following. All the footnotes are mine, put in when some elucidation of the text seemed desirable for the general reader. That on page 66 incorporates a statement in the text of the original; in translation it was easier put in a footnote, but the content is the author's. On pp. 85 and 109 the first paragraph does not appear in the French at all. The author uses Latin quotations and some implied quotations which again seemed to need elucidation. I have removed all Latin and Greek words or phrases except in a few cases where the sense needed them.

The reference on page 41 to the re-foundation of the Irish and English monasteries and the mention of Holy Cross, Melrose etc., are not in the original and are put in here for the benefit of readers who are less familiar with the French abbeys and history. Nothing has been omitted other than names.

The original idea for the translation came from Fr Cornelius Justice of Mount Melleray Abbey. I thank him for this and for his consistent interest in the project and the valuable criticisms he offered of the text. Likewise I am indebted to my fellow monk Fr Laurence Walsh of Roscrea whose careful reading of the complete text was invaluable. Fr Joseph Walsh of Mount Melleray translated the treatise in chapter 7 from the Latin, and I am in his debt for this.

I am deeply indebted to Sr Geraldine Leahy who went through the text several times and whose fluency in current French idiom and construction has been of the greatest assistance. The manuscript was read by my friends Rose Marie Doyle and Liam Maher and their expertise in English saved me from many an infelicity. Mrs Virginia Rooney and Mrs Margaret O'Brien provided excellent secretarial services.

On the American side the expert guidance of Dr Rozanne Elder of Cistercian Publications has been of inestimable benefit.

To all these good friends I am very grateful. Finally thanks to Dom Celsus Kelly for his perceptive introduction, and above all to the author, Dom André Louf, who read the entire translation in detail and made many helpful suggestions and modifications.

*Fr Nivard Kinsella*
*Roscrea, Summer 1982*

*The Cistercian Way*

# Chapter 1

## MANY PATHS — ONE WAY

In the ferment and uncertainty which followed the second Vatican Council, when religious orders and congregations were undertaking the task of renewal, a saying went the rounds among monks. It sounded like one of those wise sayings of the Desert Fathers, but you would search far among their writings before you found it. It went like this: A young monk said to a senior "What is a monk?". The senior replied "A monk is one who asks every day — What is a monk?".

Now this suggests three things: first that the definition of a monk cannot be summed up in a single sentence; second that this definition is inexhaustible and should deepen and evolve over the years; and third that a rational definition will not suffice. The reason for this last statement is that the question must indeed be put every day, and the answer can come only from living.

Another saying, this time authentically from the Fathers, seems to suggest the same idea. This is attributed to St Antony: "Every day I say to myself — Today I will begin". By now the ferment and the uncertainty have passed. Some of the solutions proposed have been less than successful, others have been painful in their application. But out of that ferment, the monastic life has emerged anew. It has come out into the light of day. We may hope that it is renewed, stripped down and pared to its essentials, and that it has thus become clearer and more attractive, especially to those who believe in the teaching of Jesus Christ. But even for those who do not believe, it is a challenge and poses questions.

However, it has not become any easier to talk about the monastic life and vocation. It remains hidden and mysterious. The monk finds this himself when he tries to talk about his life and call. Yet it has become more urgent than ever to speak about it.

Our generation is in the grip of a hunger for experience, and of a desire to live at a deeper level. In order to appease this, believer and unbeliever alike have sought new spiritual techniques and new life styles. In many respects this situation is promising. Those who believe in nothing beyond what they can see often have a deep and painful feeling that the world in which they live condemns them, despite material progress, to exist on the surface of things. They feel that unless they can find something deeper, they will be forever doomed to a life that is superficial.

But those who believe in the things of the spirit are also haunted by the same search. How can this be? Have they never tasted that God is sweet? Have the Churches never set out the treasures of life for them? Are Christians of the 20th century to be condemned to live in a spiritual vacuum?

The monastic life is one answer to this spiritual quest. It is a valid alternative even to those who do not wish to undertake it. The message of monasticism is being heard today by an increasing number of Christians, many of them young, and despite the general decline in vocations, some monastic novitiates are flourishing.

And yet, it is not at all clear that the monastic life is understood even by believers. A wide gulf exists between the life of monks and nuns in their monasteries and the outlook and interests of Christians living in the world. The quality of the monastic life as a real Christian alternative is not being questioned, or if it is, this is exceptional. The faithful generally recognise its worth and esteem it. But when it is a question of putting the monastic life into the wider context of Christian life, many, including priests, are at a loss, and seem unable to do so. We must admit that the gap between the life of monks and the ideals of an active Christianity is widening. The renewal brought about by the Council has not yet borne fruit in a better understanding for which we might legitimately have hoped. It seems we will have to wait longer for this. And in the meantime the life of monks and the life of active Christians seem to drift further and further apart.

We cannot explain this by saying that the vocabulary and life style of monks are out of date and hence incomprehensible. No doubt there is room for improvement. But language and a life style cannot become incomprehensible in a few years if there is a profound affinity between them and those of other baptised Christians. For more than fifteen centuries the two ways of life were in complete harmony. Now monastic life seems suddenly to have lost much of its credibility. There is no doubt that this situation poses urgent questions for all the Churches.

However that may be, it still remains true that for someone who wishes to deepen his life, on both the human and the Christian level, monastic life does present itself today as a genuine alternative.

Why do so many young people look to it for salvation? It would be interesting to question some of them on this. No doubt each answer would be different and each unique. Lives cannot be reduced to a common denominator.

A few people have a natural disposition for the monastic life, with its disciplined regularity. By nature reserved, meditative and reflective, they are looking for a life style which will enable them to cultivate these enriching personality traits.

Others have suddenly become aware of the profound reality of God. They realise that he is the Absolute and they feel an overpowering need of communion with him. These persons are far more numerous than is often thought. Such an experience can occur even in the most distracting life styles and often during a crisis or time of trial.

Others have met Jesus in their lives, and in a sense he has taken over their hearts. For long they have lived with the conviction that one day they will leave all things to follow him without reserve.

The sight of spiritual or material misery led others to become monks. One day they realised that it was only in this way, however strange it might seem at first sight, that they could truly become one with all those in distress and so be able to help them.

Others have already journeyed with Christ in a solitary and somewhat marginal fashion. Suddenly they feel the need of brethren to support them. They realise that they need others to lean on, and they feel they must go to a school to learn the wisdom of an ancient tradition.

Still others simply feel poverty-stricken when faced with a life which has lost a meaning for them. Unexpectedly the sign of a monastic community living together in prayer and love has revived the possibility of a joy which they thought they had lost forever.

The motives which lead young persons to knock on the door of the monastery are many. Good enough to justify the attempt, they are probably not adequate to keep them in the monastery all their lives. Most motivation needs to be examined in depth. The real motive lies beneath the surface and this must be brought to light. Only in this way will the determination to follow Christ in the monastic life be strengthened and at the same time the real meaning of the monastic life made clear. Whatever the motive that leads a young person to enter the monastery, a vocation is always an invitation which comes from God and not primarily from within oneself.

Monastic wisdom down the ages has always known this and has always held that the motives which bring a monk to the monastery are not those which keep him there. The motives which led one to enter will be tested over the years, and gradually refined and strengthened through the various crises which are the inevitable accompaniment of any serious and prolonged attempt at monastic life.

The paths leading to the monastery then are diverse. But one day they all converge and form a single Way, converging on him who said: "I am the Way" and "No one can come to the Father but by me" (Jn 14:6, 7). The Christian who becomes a monk is seeking no other way than this. What he makes his own is what he has seen and heard in the words and deeds of Jesus. As St Benedict put it in the Prologue to his *Rule*: "Let us set out on this way, with the gospel for our guide . . ." (RB, Prol. 21). In saying this St Benedict is saying no more than St John, who said: "We must live the same kind of life that Christ lived" (1 Jn 2:6).

# Chapter 2

## HISTORY OF THE MONASTIC LIFE

### 1. *In the beginning — the Word*

Jesus Christ did not directly found the monastic life, but it did have its origins in his preaching, for this included those elements which later became characteristic of the way of life of monks. Did Jesus not tell us that "we must leave all to follow him" (Mk 10:28), that "we must sell our possessions and give to the poor" (Mt 19:21), and that we must "renounce marriage for the sake of the kingdom" (Mt 19:12)? Did not Jesus surround himself with men and women disciples who shared his everyday life and his care for the coming of the kingdom, and especially his mysterious dialogue with the Father?

Jesus appeared to his contemporaries as the equal of those great men of the Old Testament who had been suddenly uprooted from their ordinary lives by the power of the word of God, so that they might be more completely dedicated to God's service—men such as Abraham, Moses and the prophets. From the beginning of sacred history, the word of God has never ceased to work in this way. It calls each one, inviting him in a way special to him and dedicating him to a particular service. The word of God re-creates a man from the very depths of his being—if necessary even changing his name (Gen 17:5). In this way, through the call of one individual, the life of a whole people can be profoundly changed and they can be led to God.

But always at the beginning is the Word. It is the same Word which inspired the prophets and leaders of the Jewish people, the same Word that was finally incarnated, without loss or diminution, in the beloved Son, our Lord Jesus Christ. At the beginning of every Christian life is the word of the Lord. It comes in many ways, but it always calls accepted values and standards into question and stirs the soul of the believer to its depths. St Antony the Great, the father of monks, owed his vocation to a word of the gospel, heard by chance during a celebration of the eucharist one day: "If you wish to go the whole way, go, sell your possessions, and give to the poor, and then you will have riches in heaven; and come, follow me" (Mt 19:21). Antony did not know where this would lead him, because at the beginning of the fourth century, no one, at least in Egypt, had lived the kind of solitary life to which this drew him. But the word of Jesus suddenly coming alive in his heart was call enough. On the strength of it, he committed his whole life.

Likewise two centuries later, St Benedict, who was to become the Patriarch of the monks of the West, did not know any other way than that of the Gospel. In the Prologue to his *Rule* he says this to his disciples: "Clothed then with faith and the performance of good works, let us set out on this way, with the Gospel for our guide, that we may deserve to see him who has called us to his kingdom" (RB, Prol. 21). St Benedict knew that his *Rule* could not supplant the Gospel. On the contrary, when he wrote the final chapter, he recalled that the *Rule* is only a sort of humble beginning, a kind of manual of introduction to what he calls "the heights of perfection, the loftier summits of teaching and virtue", which the disciple will find on every page of the Scriptures (cf RB 73). We could say that St Benedict in writing the *Rule*, has to some extent effaced himself before the Gospel. The Word of God is the sole rule of life and it alone is more than adequate. Any religious rule has meaning only to the extent that it can make the demands of the Word of God specific. It must apply the Gospel to the concrete circumstances of a particular age and culture. It is as though the Word came alight for the founder at a particular time in history, and he is then able to maintain this light for those who come after him. This is not something that is "given" beforehand. St Benedict knew nothing of the world-wide destiny of his *Rule*. He was content to prepare his monks to hear the word of the Gospel and to follow Christ.

The second Vatican Council took up these same ideas when it recalled in a profound phrase: "Since the final norm of the religious life is the following of Christ as the gospel puts it before us, this must be taken by all institutes as the supreme rule"[1].

## 2. *The Word passed on to others*

From the very beginning of the Christian community, we see a special way of life being adopted by some men and women. Its outstanding feature is celibacy for the sake of the Kingdom, or for love of Christ. The original word used to describe these people in Aramaic meant "solitary", and this referred to their choice of celibacy. Likewise in Greek the word *monachos*, with much the same meaning, was used. This word came into English as "monk". The solitaries were noted for their assiduity at prayer, whether in the church or at home. They had a place reserved for them in the church, and certain offices of prayer at night and in the morning were unique to them. They interrupted their sleep in order to pray, and they fasted more frequently than others.

They were also known for their exceptional welcome for the poor. Sometimes the diaconate or the most exacting ministries of charity were entrusted to them. They were called virgins or widows if they were women, and ascetics if they were men. There is nothing grim or forbidding about this latter word. Literally it means simply someone in training. An ascetic is a Christian who is totally committed to his vocation, and whose entire life and activity are dominated by the fact of his being a Christian.

During the first three centuries the ascetics lived as part of the parish community. Sometimes they occupied a special place in the church, but in the beginning they did not live in community. Either they lived alone, or if they were young, with their parents at home. Small communities gradually began to be formed, generally of one sex. The early Councils also attest to the existence of couples dedicated to the ascetical life, but on the whole this was considered a dangerous practice and the Councils were against it.

In the first half of the fourth century, shortly before the persecutions temporarily abated, the ascetics began to leave the Christian communities to live in complete solitude. They withdrew to the desert or to the mountains. A Syrian document of the period calls them "mountain-dwellers", and this was to reprove the practice of living alone which was considered incompatible with the Christian's need to belong to a community where the liturgy could be celebrated.

This condemnation is not surprising. A new and unusual way of life in the community could hardly be unanimously welcomed and approved right from its first appearance. Great bishops hesitated about what course to take. St Basil of Ceasarea, who was later to bring order to an ascetical movement shaken by suspect extravagances, managed to write a monastic rule without ever using the word "monk"! For him the word was still suspect.

But other bishops and theologians readily defended the solitaries, for example Theodoret of Cyr in his *Religious History*. In the churches of the Syrian language, St Ephraim sang of the marvels of the solitary liturgy, invisibly linked to that celebrated in all the churches where the faithful were united in worship. At Alexandria, the life of St Antony, written by St Athanasius, became one of the religious bestsellers of the era, and was regarded as the official eulogy of the solitary life.

It was at this time that the title "monk" (*monachos*) was definitively adopted. It seems that its primitive meaning of celibate was forgotten and it was interpreted henceforth as solitary or alone. Others interpreted it as meaning "one" or "unified" in the sense that a person who became a monk has succeeded in unifying his being, fragmented by sin.

It was not only in Egypt that the monks adopted the solitary life. It happened also in Syria, Mesopotamia, Palestine, Sinai and Byzantium. While it is true that St Antony became the Father of monks, there were many others equally famous. We find their names in ancient monastic literature—men such as Macarius, Arsenius, Moses and Poemen, to mention only a few.

Not all monks were solitaries. From the beginning of primitive monasticism several tendencies developed within it. The effort to maintain these conflicting tendencies in balance, coupled with the creative tension between them, has been one of the most powerful forces in the evolution of the monastic life at every era in its history.

From earliest times groups of ascetics lived in community. Without leaving the town or village they remained part of the local church. The reforming zeal of St Basil would later be directed to the better organisation of such communities. But even the solitaries in the desert did not consider solitude an absolute. They always admitted disciples who came to put themselves under their direction. It was St Pachomius who organised this movement to community on a grander scale, so that he has come to be regarded as the father of community life for monks. He worked out a life style which enabled men to pursue the absolute search for God in a community of brethren. Thus Pachomius became one of the founders of the way of life we call cenobitic — a life devoted to seeking God in a community.

The relationship between life in community and the life of the hermit was not always easy to determine. In some places, for example in Egypt, the two ways of life developed more or less parallel without influencing each other to any significant extent. There was some rivalry between them and people asked which of the two was better and more likely to lead them to holiness. The works of John Cassian have preserved traces of this questioning.

In other places the identity and inner dymanic of each form of life gradually emerged. Thus life in community was considered to be for beginners, while the life of the hermit was for the more advanced. This was the case in Palestine and Mesopotamia. But in Asia Minor St Basil and St Gregory of Nyssa took a different line. They held that even the highest mystical experience is within the reach of every monk, whether he lives in community or is a hermit, provided he is ready to undergo the purification which the Holy Spirit would certainly demand of him.

Monasticism of both types spread rapidly in East and West during the fourth and fifth centuries. All the Churches had their great solitaries and famous monasteries. These latter were often made famous by the public approval and patronage given them by such great bishops as Ambrose of Milan, Hilary of Poitiers, Martin of Tours, Augustine of Hippo, and so many others.

27

### 3. *A developing identity*

The identity of the monastic life gradually emerged from the ascetical movement in the Church. The ascetics remained part of the local Church and its structures, but the monk withdrew into solitude. The degree of this solitude could vary considerably. At one end of the spectrum was the hermit or recluse, living in a remote desert. At the other end was the great monastery around which a city often grew up. The separation here between the town and the monastery was only the enclosure wall, and sometimes this was as much symbolic as real. Nevertheless it was carefully maintained.

Not that all contact with the world was broken. The people of God came to the monastery and even though the monk did not seek this contact, he had to give them the encouragement and the help of his prayer. They came to the monk because they felt that he had the Word of God, and even though he might wish for solitude he had to dispense this Word to God's people.

But while he sought to be alone, the monk soon found himself with other like-minded men. The search for God is not to be undertaken alone or on one's own initiative. Monastic life is a living faith transmitted from brother to brother. In order to learn it, a man must immerse himself in the stream of living tradition, and must drink of its wisdom. The most ancient monastic literature consists of a collection of sayings attributed to the Desert Fathers. These are generally couched in the form of answers to questions put by disciples. The teacher was usually called *"Abba"* if a man and *"Amma"* if a woman. *Abba* is an Aramaic word for father, and its very early appearance in this context shows that it was used by the first Christian communities, before the use of Greek became wisespread in the Church.

The monastic life was thought of as a living entity in which wise men would beget spiritual sons. Their words were seen as a true source of life for others, and they thus came to be called *Abba* or *Amma*. Their wise sayings were passed on to others, at first orally, and later in writing. Collections of these sayings, or "sentences" as they were called, gradually took shape and came to be regarded as rules of life, into which the *Abba* had put all his wisdom and experience for the benefit of future disciples. In the West to this day, the superior of a monastery is called "abbot", which is the same word as *Abba*. Thus each abbot takes his place in the long succession of seniors and teachers who have transmitted the monastic life from one generation to another, and have taught others the experience to which it leads.

As well as having an abbot or spiritual father, the monk also has brothers in community, unless he is a hermit. He can rely on their affectionate support. Without his being aware of it, he will be formed by the spirit of this community which he joins. He will share in this spirit and make it his own. Each community has a particular way of expressing the monastic charism, and this impregnates every aspect of its life. Each of the brethren has a special word to say to the others. This word may never be spoken orally, because it belongs to another order of being. It is communicated by a person's attentive presence to the others, or by the example he gives. In this way not only the abbot but every monk in the community guarantees the quality of the life to the newcomer. He needs this guarantee for he has left all things to come to the monastic life. Thus through the brethren as well as through the abbot the rule remains life-giving today.

## 4. *St Benedict*

About two centuries after St Antony, at the end of the first great period of monastic history, St Benedict of Nursia appears. He was born in the year 480 and died about the year 547. While still young Benedict was sent to Rome to complete his education. Finding life in the city little to his taste, he left and went to live in solitude near Subiaco. After a short while he was found there by some shepherds, and soon disciples came to put themselves under his direction. Benedict grouped these in small communities of about a dozen monks, scattered around the hillsides above Subiaco. When circumstances forced him to leave the place, he went south and founded a monastery at Cassino. There he lived for the remainder of his life and there he wrote his *Rule for Monks*.

Benedict had no pretensions to being a founder. He merely wrote a rule of life for the little community which depended on him. He did not set out to write an original work. He was inspired in large measure by a recent work which is now known as the *Rule of the Master*, so called because we do not know who wrote it. It seems to have been written in northern Italy or southern Gaul about the year 500. The author collected the traditions of monastic life and adapted them to the place where he was living and writing.

St Benedict in his turn also adapted. Where the Master is long-winded, Benedict is concise. He has nuanced and highlighted the sayings of the Master, which reflect a somewhat doctrinaire theology. He has softened a rigidity in the Master's work. But above all he has centered the life of the monk on the person of Christ. He speaks of the love which the monk owes Christ — 'The love of Christ must come before all else" (RB 4:21). St Benedict found that phrase in the *Rule of the Master*, but he gives it and the idea it embodies a centrality and importance that the Master does not.

Benedict also knew other monastic sources, but he used them differently from the Master. He may have used St Pachomius but he certainly used St Augustine. One of the latter's great contributions to monastic life is his emphasis on the presence of the brethren and the support which love finds in a monastic community.

Benedict is wide-ranging in his use of sources and likes to refer to the whole monastic tradition. He quotes "Our Holy Father St Basil" and recommends his monks to read the works of Basil (RB 73). He orders that every day some parts of the writings of John Cassian be read in public in the community or something from the sayings of the Desert Fathers (RB 42:3). It would be a mistake however to see the *Rule* as no more than a collection of various passages taken from the older monastic writers. Benedict imposed a unity on his sources and put them together in such a way that he produced the single most powerful and influential document of the monastic tradition in the western Church. His *Rule* carries the imprint of that grace which was personal to himself.

In addition special attention must be given to the virtue of discretion, which permeates the whole *Rule*. Today we would call it discernment. This is neither natural caution nor prudent moderation, but a kind of insight which enables the abbot to adjust the demands of the monastic life to the grace which is given either to the community as a whole or to the individual monk. St Benedict calls this disposition the mother of all the virtues (RB 64:19) and urges it on the abbot. He is deeply convinced that everyone has his own gift from God, one in this way and another in that (RB 40:1). He wishes that we should neither anticipate the action of grace nor try to go beyond where it leads us. Grace is not at the disposal of anyone, even of the abbot. When it is given it will lead the monk well beyond anything attainable by his own powers and strength. In speaking of the action of grace, and the advance of the monk in the spiritual life, St Benedict uses the phrase, "our hearts overflowing with the inexpressible delight of love" (RB, Prol.49). Such love is a sure sign of the action of the Holy Spirit.

## 5. *A rule for today*

The *Rule of St Benedict* was not immediately adopted by all monks. There were other rules and some of these continued in use, but eventually only St Benedict's survived for monks and that of St Augustine for clerics living in community. The universal acceptance of the *Rule of St Benedict* was due to the influence of Charlemagne and his son Louis the Pious. At the Council of Aix-la-Chapelle in 817, the *Rule* was made obligatory on all monks in the Empire. Within two centuries the *Rule* had already made its impact and held the promise of the long history which lay ahead of it.

But this history itself poses a problem. The *Rule of St Benedict* was written for a particular locality at the beginning of the sixth century. What can it say to us — peoples so different to those of St Benedict's day, living in places so different to his central Italy, and in cultures so far removed from his?

This problem is more acute in so far as the greater number of monastic reforms down the centuries have presented themselves as reforms precisely by appealing to the *Rule*. They have all more or less sought to return to the *Rule*. Charlemagne imposed it on the monasteries of his dominions because he considered that in it the monks had an efficacious instrument of reform. Later other reformers, including those of Cîteaux, thought the same. Each time the *Rule* appeared as a word of salvation which could lead to conversion.

This special place given to an ancient rule is a phenomenon peculiar to monasticism. To understand it, it is not enough to say that the text of the *Rule* contains a summary of the principles of the monastic life. Neither is it enough to claim that it faithfully traces the main characteristics of the kind of life that history has considered to be authentically monastic. The *Rule* is always more than a code of life or a manual of doctrine, although it is both of these. It is above all a resumé of a spiritual experience that lies at the heart of monastic life. The principles of doctrine it evokes, or the details of observance which are recommended or even imposed by it, have an inner power. This power is an experience of the very life of God in Christ Jesus and his Holy Spirit. No rule has any other meaning than to be this path of life, as indeed the Prologue says (RB, Prol.20).

When St Benedict wrote his rule he was there in person to comment on it in his own words, to show through his example how it should be lived, and to demonstrate through his own government of the monastery how it should be used in practice. The monks had not only the letter of the *Rule*, but also the person of St Benedict, on whom, as his biographer St Gregory says, "rested the spirit of all the just" (Dial.8). The words of the *Rule* came alive through his presence. Life was transmitted simultaneously by the written rule and by the living word of the saint in his own life and teaching. This is the only way in which words of life can be transmitted by a rule. The words of the rule always carry more than their literal meaning and must be interpreted by a living teacher.

After the death of St Benedict, his monks still needed this living teaching. Other abbots succeeded him and the communities them-selves were living. In them young and old lived together, and passed on the rule to one another, often without being aware of it. In this way the rule has never been a dead letter. Across the generations of abbots and monks it has acquired a living face. It has been a source of life for them, giving life to each succeeding generation. In this way it has inspired successive reforms which are the very stuff of monastic history.

The letter of the *Rule* contains life within itself, and this life can be awakened in the heart of the disciple who listens. Hence the importance of the very opening words of the *Rule*: "Listen, my son". St Benedict wrote the *Rule* from his own personal experience and in doing so he filled the words of his book with life, for he filled them with the knowledge that comes from living. Down the centuries countless monks have drawn life from these words, through the action of their communities which have begotten them in the Spirit, and especially through the seniors who have taught them the meaning of these words.

The *Rule* is like a treasure which can never be fully exploited. No single generation of monks can exhaust all its riches. Not only does it go back to St Benedict and the Desert Fathers, but it is in a certain sense an element at the very heart of the Church, contributing to its full life, even though in a hidden and unseen fashion. Reforms succeed each other down the centuries, and none is ever quite the same as those preceding it. Certain gospel charisms always remain essential to the monastic life. Their expression however can vary and so can the emphasis given them. Each epoch and each church brings forth that form of monastic life which best expresses its own grace. Some details of observance last for centuries, others quickly fall into disuse. This does not matter. Their ultimate value is not in themselves but in their power to transmit a spiritual experience. Thanks to this experience, the *Rule* remains always living and vital. A reform is only a new re-reading of the text. This modern word "re-reading" describes well what happens as each generation of monks takes up the *Rule* anew. The text passes from one generation to another, from hand to hand and from heart to heart. Gradually and imperceptibly all its potential and depth are brought to light.

## 6. *The reform of Cîteaux*

During the eleventh century a number of reforms stirred the monastic world. One of the most successful was Cluny, which gave new life to the Benedictine family. But it was only one among many. This time also saw the emergence of several monastic institutes which have lasted until our own day, such as the Camaldolese, the Carthusians and the Cistercians. All these reforms had certain traits in common, mostly borrowed from the spiritual aspirations of their age. Notable among these was a pronounced taste for solitude on the margin of existing institutions, and an attempt to return to the Gospel.

Society in the eleventh century was in a state of ferment. Its various currents needed to be purified if they were to be used in renewing the ancient monastic tradition. Cîteaux managed to do this in a way that was peculiar to itself. In the diocese of Langres in Burgundy was a Benedictine monastery called Molesmes. Under the leadership of its abbot Robert, it had already accepted a reform. In the year 1098 Robert led twenty-one monks out of Molesmes to found a new reformed monastery. This was Cîteaux in the neighbouring diocese of Chalons. The most ancient documents of Cîteaux tell us that the desire of these men was to seek God in a desert place, in true poverty, in real independence of the secular establishment, and in greater fidelity to the *Rule of St Benedict*. It seems likely that the example of the Desert Fathers who had lived before St Benedict also influenced the project.

The beginnings were difficult. In particular they were marked by a lack of understanding on the part of the brethren who remained at Molesmes. These obtained a decree from the pope ordering Robert to return to Molesmes at the end of the first year. He was succeeded at Cîteaux by Alberic. Recruitment seemed uncertain, and so the reformers faced the future with no other hope than the belief that they were doing God's will. The community seemed doomed because no one was joining it. In the words of the *Exordium*, one of the oldest documents of the Order: "it caused sorrow and distress to the aforementioned abbot and monks that in those days only rarely did anyone come there in order to follow after them. For these holy men longed to hand down to their successors for the future benefit of many this treasure of virtues which they had received from heaven. Yet almost all those who saw or learned about the unusual and almost unheard-of rigour of their lives, instead of approaching them, hastened to avoid them in both spirit and body, nor did they cease from doubting in the ability of the monks to persevere"[2].

It was in this uncertainty that Alberic died. He had for successor "a certain brother by the name of Stephen, an Englishman by nationality . . . a lover of the rule and of the place"[3].

The monks did not want to reduce in any way the austerity of their way of life. They prized even more highly the exact observance of the *Rule of St Benedict*. Under the abbacy of Stephen, "the brethren and abbot prohibited the Duke of that land (i.e. Burgundy) or any lord from holding his court at any time in that monastery, as they used on their part to do on the occasion of great feasts"[4]. Furthermore, they decided to suppress everything "that savoured of pride or superfluity, or that would ever corrupt poverty, the safeguard of virtue, which they had chosen of their own freewill"[5].

Therefore "in those days God visited that place and showed forth his deepest mercy to the brethren who implored him, who cried out to him, and who wept before him, who day and night groaned long and deep, who drew near to the brink of despair because they had almost no successors. For now the grace of God sent to that monastery so many literate and noble clerics, and laymen who were as powerful as they were distinguished in the world, that at one time thirty men eagerly entered the novitiate"[6].

Among these, or rather at their head, was Bernard of Clairvaux. The expansion of Cîteaux had begun.

## 7. *The spread of the Cistercians*

With the entry of Bernard to Cîteaux in 1112 the new monastery soon experienced a period of extraordinary expansion. Foundations multiplied at an ever-increasing rate. In 1113 La Ferté was founded, in 1114 Pontigny, and in 1115 Clairvaux was founded with Bernard as its abbot. A month later saw the foundation of Morimond, in Germany. By 1140 there were no less than ten foundations a year, and ten years later, in 1150, this had increased to twenty a year. At the time of St Bernard's death in 1153 the Order counted 339 houses. Fortunately, in the person of Stephen Harding, its third abbot, the mother house at Cîteaux had found an organiser of genius who was able to maintain unity and communion in the organisation during this time of incredibly rapid growth. To achieve this, Stephen drew up a document which was approved by all the abbots of the Order. It was called the *Charter of Charity*, "for its whole content so breathed love that almost nothing else is seen to be treated there than this "Owe no man anything except to love one another" (Rom. 13:8)"[7].

The great contribution which this strikingly original document made to monastic life was to set up a new kind of organisation between monasteries. Less centralised than that of Cluny, it was based on the maintenance of links between mother-house and daughter-house. These links were to be both supportive and challenging. The rights and duties of each house were clearly described. The abbot of the mother house had to visit the daughter house each year to see if anything needed improvement. Each year also, all the abbots had to meet at Cîteaux, the Mother of the Order, in order to discuss the observance which must be so regulated in every monastery that it reflected the way the rule was understood at Cîteaux. This meeting was the General Chapter, an institution which inspired other religious orders, and which eventually became widespread in the Church. It was in the General Chapter that the abbots could periodically examine their re-reading of the *Rule of St Benedict*, and thus gradually promote a common understanding of it. Out of this arose a true Cistercian tradition which would maintain its genuine originality through all subsequent evolution and change.

Besides those wise and prudent organisers who laid the juridical foundations for the new institute, Cîteaux also produced an impressive number of spiritual writers. Among them is Bernard of Clairvaux, the greatest of his century. He would later be called the last of the Fathers. It would seem that the novitiate at Cîteaux attracted some of the best minds of the period. These young men had been formed by the spiritual currents of their own era. Now with the experience of monastic life behind them they were able to dialogue with the spirituality of their time. They lived at the dawn of Scholasticism and in general they found this too intellectual for their taste. They drew eagerly and fully from the treasures put at their disposal during the long hours of *Lectio divina*. The teaching of the Fathers was assimilated by them in a new way. The abbots too set themselves to the task of teaching this doctrine to their monks. Daily they spoke to their communities and thus daily they passed on to them the wisdom of the monastic tradition. The abbots were often the intellectual élite of the Order. They eagerly explored and examined everything that might throw light on the way of love on which they were engaged.

The Cistercian monasteries of the time claimed to be "schools of charity", that is places where one could learn the secrets of divine love and of mutual love between the brethren. Among the texts of Scripture which were endlessly commented on was the Canticle of Canticles, that marvellous love song which has survived the centuries, and with the help of which the mystics have celebrated the joys of intimacy between Christ and his Church and between him and the soul of every believer.

At this same time men's minds were opening to the East, thanks to the recent translations of the Greek Fathers which had begun to circulate. Most of the Cistercian writers had read some of the Greek Fathers. Among the most notable Greeks were Origen and Maximus the Confessor, and these the Cistercians used with flair and originality. Was not St Bernard himself confronted in his community by the murmurs of some of his monks who were

37

unhappy because their abbot was quoting the heretical Doctor of Alexandria? (cf St Bernard, *Ser. de Div.*, 34:1). Wishing to explore the ways of love, the early Cistercians examined the human soul in depth, for it is the soul which will be transformed by these experiences.

In order to understand love better, they had to plumb more deeply the hidden potential of man. The Cistercians were psychologists before the term was coined and they undertook this study with truly exceptional curiosity. Many of them wrote a Treatise on the Soul (*De Anima*) under one form or another. They studied the nature of the soul, its original fall, the laws and ways of its restoration in Christ, and the degrees of love. And they did this systematically and methodically.

In this way a body of doctrine has come down to us from the twelfth century which remains the basis of Cistercian life as it has developed over the centuries. Its characteristic traits are always found at any era of the Order's history. These include a love of the word of God, the mirror in which the monk tries to decipher the meaning of his daily life; a tender devotion to the person of Jesus Christ, the Word Incarnate; an effort by the monk to reproduce in his own life the mysteries of Christ's earthly life, through which will be revealed the invisible Word living in the glory of the Father.

The monk is devoted to the Virgin Mary, still today as in past ages the Mother of the Word—in his Church and in contemplative hearts. He cultivates a taste for a life that is interior, for as St Bernard says, the more interior it is, the more attractive he finds it. The monk must build an interior mansion or cell in his heart, to which he ceaselessly returns in order to find the hidden presence of God. And having found it he remains there in loving contemplation. The Cistercian monk tries to live in deep peace even amid the distractions of the common life.

In the second half of the twelfth century, the literary output of the Cistercians was so considerable that we can correctly speak of a "Cistercian School". The themes of this school, taken from the great tradition of the Fathers, are treated with striking originality and with a vocabulary peculiar to the Cistercians. St Bernard is its indisputable master. His friend William of St-Thierry, long a Benedictine abbot before taking the Cistercian habit, follows him closely and sometimes surpasses him in the sharpness of his theological vision. The English Cistercians celebrated Aelred of Rievaulx as the peer of Bernard. Aelred treated many of the same themes as Bernard, and did so with great warmth and in a very personal fashion of his own. Another disciple of Bernard was Guerric, a former scholar of Tournai, who exchanged the dry scholasticism of the age for the piquant and savoury language of Bernard. Guerric succeeded in integrating his experiences in a biblical vocabulary of great richness and exegetical precision, which at times verges on poetry. Others too must be cited. There were Isaac of Stella, a metaphysician who broke with the researches of his age to become a monk; Gilbert of Hoyland who took up the commentary on the Canticle where St Bernard left it unfinished at his death, but who in turn died before completing the task; and Baldwin who outlined a perceptive theology of the cenobitic life.

## 8. *From Cîteaux to our own day*

The historians of the Order have presented the twelfth century as its Golden Age. This was true especially of France, but in the Low Countries and Germany the Golden Age came in the fourteenth and fifteenth centuries and in Spain it came later still. Gradually signs of decline appeared. Poverty and austerity of life were no longer prized. Factors external to the monastic life compromised its fervour. Notable among these were the Wars of Religion and the *Commendam*, a system whereby men who were not monks were appointed abbots and drew the revenues of the monastery while caring nothing for its life and observance. It would however be incorrect to use the word decadence to describe the situation. While there may have been laxity in some particular monasteries there was no general decadence. As soon as a real need was felt reform movements arose from the fifteenth century on. These were often the work of one outstanding personality who undertook a local reform. If this succeeded, other monasteries followed suit, if necessary asking the reformer to come and help them, or putting themselves under his direction. In this way new links and groupings formed within the Order, sometimes with unhappy results as reformed and non-reformed monasteries opposed each other.

The tensions between these two concepts of the Cistercian life have furnished pages of history which are both glorious and sad. Some reforms were exemplary, but had only a limited life. Among them all only one has survived up to the present time: that of La Trappe, an abbey in France. In 1638, Armand Jean le Bouthillier, Abbé de Rancé, aged twelve, was appointed abbot *in commendam* of La Trappe. This meant that he could live on the revenues of the abbey but need never even visit it. Normally such an abbot appointed a prior to run the monastery and took little further interest in it. With Rancé it was not so. When he reached adulthood, he was ordained, and decided that the state of religion was such that he had a duty to assume the office of abbot of this ancient abbey. So he joined the Cistercians, did a novitiate, and was installed as abbot of the monastery. He was a man of powerful personality and wide monastic culture. His reading embraced the best in the tradition of both Eastern and Western monasticism. His literary activity, both as a polemicist and as a spiritual writer, brought the reform a degree of publicity which helped ensure its permanence and success. In the end other reforms aligned themselves with La Trappe which became synonymous with the Strict Observance.

At the end of the seventeenth century and all during the eighteenth until the French Revolution, the ascetisicm of La Trappe offered a sort of evangelical and often successful antidote to the excesses of the age and the hidden canker of society. The refinement of that society was matched only by its corruption, and the holiness of La Trappe shines out against this. The courage and the rigorous austerity of the monks did not entirely correspond to the discretion of St Benedict, nor were they always completely in harmony with the mystical fervour of the first Cistercians. The reform of La Trappe reproduced too literally the austerity of some forms of primitive monasticism. In this way it was very much part of its age, which was one of noble and passionate extremes.

However, La Trappe survived its age, and also survived the

Revolution. This latter led to the closure of the Abbey, but the community escaped and survived and through this fact the Strict Observance itself was to survive.

As soon as La Trappe was suppressed in 1791, the novice-master Dom Augustin de Lestrange led twenty-four religious to an abandoned Carthusian monastery in Switzerland, called Val Sainte. With the spread of French power later he was forced to leave Val Sainte, and he led the monks in a scarcely credible odyssey across Austria, Poland, Russia and Germany seeking refuge. At the same time he sent monks to found new houses in America, Belgium and Germany. In 1815 when return to France became possible the monks of Lestrange's group, now called Trappists, set themselves to the work of re-occupying some of the ancient abbeys. In this way through a circumstance that now seems providential, continuity with the medieval past was assured, and the return of the monks to Ireland and England from which they had been expelled at the time of the Reformation, was begun. In 1832 Mount Melleray in Ireland was founded from Melleray near Nantes, and from its line of descent are numbered nine abbeys of monks today in Ireland, England, the United States and Australasia.

Thus through the torment of the Revolution a new expansion of the Cistercian life began. It drew its strength from the reform which Dom Augustine succeeded in imposing on the communities which he founded.

Lestrange's rigorism and austerity yielded nothing to that of Abbot de Rancé. In fact it surpassed it. Private rooms disappeared, and the full common life was restored. Privations in food and sleep increased to such an extent that on more than one occasion Rome hesitated or simply refused to approve them. The daily life of the monk was minutely regulated and his timetable arranged in such detail that he could consider himself as always in a state of total dependence on the will of God. In fact a deep devotion to the will of God was one of the most salient spiritual traits of this reform. The monk was asked to sacrifice himself endlessly to repair the ravages of evil in the Church and in the kingdom. This spirit of reparation in homage to the majesty of God explains in part the

41

great severity which marked this current of monastic life right up to the beginning of this century.

For several decades the Trappists (as those who now followed the reform of La Trappe were called) formed three groupings, each following a slightly different version of the regulations of either De Rancé or Lestrange. There was little real difference between them. In 1892, at the invitation of the Holy See, the three congregations re-united in one General Chapter and under one Superior General to form the Order of Cistercians of the Strict Observance. This union was itself a blessing, and it signalled a new deepening of the spiritual life. Little by little, the austerity inherited from La Trappe and especially from Val Sainte, was reduced to its proper place. Thanks to the re-discovery of sources and of the Cistercian authors of the twelfth century, attention was once more focused on the Bible and on liturgical and interior prayer.

The years which followed the second World War brought a new grace, an extraordinary expansion of the Order outside Europe, notably in America but also in Africa, Australia and Japan. This meant that the General Chapter had to tackle the problem of adapting the monastic life to different cultures even before the second Vatican Council. Already at this time the Chapter had taken some specific initiatives—lessening vocal prayer and toning down austerities.

In this way the Order found itself well prepared to undertake the double task which the second Vatican Council imposed on all religious; to bring about renewal by returning more faithfully to the spirit of the founders, and to adapt the expressions of this spirit to the demands of our time. Several General Chapters devoted themselves to this work. The structures of the Order became more pliable, and responsibility for major decisions fell back more to the local abbot in co-operation with his community. The liturgy was renewed in order to create a community prayer which was simpler and if possible more contemplative, more suited to provide immediate initiation into interior contemplation. Work was organised to ensure to each monk the leisure necessary for reading the Word of God, and for prayer. The essential demands of monastic life were not reduced. The Chapters sought rather to highlight them and to deepen the monk's awareness of their true meaning and value. In order to do this some observances were sacrificed. Quantity had sometimes to be sacrificed to quality.

Above all there has been an attempt to restore the formative power of the monastic life itself for the monk. The ancient fathers had always been aware of this and had believed in it. But if the life itself is to form the monk and to teach him the ways of God, then it must be adapted patiently and pliably to the work of grace in each one, and to the potential of each individual. Nowadays there is less tendency to impose a uniform life style, worked out in advance, on everyone. The aim is rather to stir up and nourish an interior liberty by which the Holy Spirit anticipates the work of man.

This process is by no means ended yet. This book reflects something of the present state of monastic life. Only future generations will be able to say whether the present renewal has been the beginning of a new spiritual flowering or if, badly conceived and wrongly interpreted, it has unwittingly caused a weakening of the grace it was meant to strengthen. Either way, Cistercians today are trying to be faithful to the spirit of their fathers of the twelfth century, and in this way they will be faithful to the spirit of St Benedict and the monastic tradition which preceded him. The programme of life left by the fathers of Cîteaux has been reformulated for the present generation in clear and powerful fashion by the General Chapter of 1969, in two major documents. These are the *Declaration on the Cistercian Life* and the *Statute on Unity and Pluralism*. They are of capital importance for an understanding of the evolution of the Order today. (They will be found in Appendix A.)

# Chapter 3

## THE FIRST STEPS

### 1. *"To Leave the World"*

To become a Cistercian is to undertake to live in a specific place, which is the monastery. It also implies that "we leave the world", to use the traditional phrase. What this means in effect is that we leave behind all those ties which have been part of our lives up to now. We must leave our families, our parents, our brothers and sisters, and our friends. We will no longer live in the family home or meet our friends in those places with which we have been so familiar. We are attracted by another place, not by its appearance but by its ethos and spirit.

These speak to us of a presence, of someone who lives there, who has made his dwelling in this place and now he invites us to join him, to dwell with him. He has chosen the men who are here and has given them to one another as brothers. If these new ties are to grow, we must distance ourselves from the others we love. It may even seem to us that in the effort to do this, our heart dies, and remains apparently lifeless for a long time. But it will grow strong in this trial, and will find both family and friends again in a deeper and more abiding union. For that union will be enriched with the newness of God and we will love again in a truly new communion of spirit. However, this separation from family and friends, even though genuinely desired and sought, is painful. It involves saying goodbye to those we love, and entering a new world, a new way of life, a whole new set of relationships.

This is the first experience of what is called "cloister". It sets the bounds of this place, is its distinguishing characteristic, and lends an air of mystery to the monastery and its life. No one can understand the meaning of cloister with its solitude and aloneness unless he comes to the monastery on more than a passing visit.

If he is to understand it he must come to live there. A person who comes to join the monastery does this because he has chosen the place and he wishes to be faithful to the cloister. The Lord who dwells here will not allow his search for God to end in failure. Perhaps later on the aspirant will feel that he has in fact failed to find God in the monastery, and decide to leave. If this happens, the very shape and appearance of the cloister, speaking to him as it does of peace and prayer and rest in God, will recall him to his purpose, and in this he will hear the last appeal of his Lord. The very stones will speak to him.

*Another World.* The newness of this little world soon wears off, however, and the newcomer gets to know his way around. In the case of some monasteries the confines are narrow and the extent of their lands small. We are indeed fortunate if the place retains its newness and attractiveness for us always. There are some places which retain a beauty at which we always marvel—the power of the mountains, the majesty of great lakes or the secret life of the deep forests.

The community there has a character of its own. This group of monks or nuns has inherited a whole tradition and this is so even if the monastery is only recently founded. It incarnates its own spirit in a life style both old and new, and to a large extent it is through this life style that the community spirit is passed on to others.

## 2. *A Day in the monk's life*

The most notable difference in life style is the time of going to bed and of rising. Instead of going to bed very late at night or even in the early hours of the morning, the monk is called to go to sleep by the evening Angelus bell, although it is scarcely eight o'clock when it rings. Next morning at a very early hour, perhaps as early as 3.15, a loud insistent bell will call him from sleep. The monk's vigil begins as that of the world ends. The newcomer must follow the community as best he can. The monastery church welcomes him. To it he will come seven times a day to chant the praise of God. And even during the night he will come to sing to God, whom no eye has ever seen, but who draws near in silence.

Cistercian monks hold to this nocturnal prayer. They have undertaken to chant their first office before sunrise. In the silence of the night they are at their Lord's disposal. "O Lord open my lips and my mouth will declare your praise". All together they sing a hymn to God. A long series of psalms is divided into two sections, each about a quarter of an hour long and each followed by a reading. The first reading is from the Bible, the second from a commentary by a church Father or some other spiritual writer. At this hour when the thousand occupations of the day do not trouble one's spirit, there is effectively no other alternative than prayer. And if one's heart is awake, sleep does not appear as a real alternative.

After this a long period is left at the disposal of each. This is the best time for each to turn in his own way to God. Each has his own rhythm, his own place, and especially his own way of making himself present to God. One of the ways used by all monks is *lectio divina*. Monks prefer this old Latin term to anything modern, as the modern term "spiritual reading" does not denote the same thing at all. *Lectio* for the monk means reading the word of God in a slow meditative way so that it may take root in the heart and germinate there. The first condition for this is that he give it time, and this time when night ensures quiet and calm is best of all. At night even the slightest whisper can be heard, the faintest echo or the quietest word is audible. But the silence of the night is more than an invitation. It is also a symbol of that silence we must create within us, in which God speaks or keeps silence like the closest of friends.

The office of Lauds brings the community together once again to sing of the greatness of God at the hour of the sun's rising. A festive joyfulness permeates this office and each monk tries to put himself in harmony with its spirit. Lauds is usually followed by mass, the celebration of the daily eucharist. The community is the Body of Christ and each one learns anew from the Lord that he is a member of this one Body, bound to all those assembled with him in the peace of Christ. This is the heart of the life, and it cannot be affected by the little ups and downs of every day, the small frictions that inevitably occur between the brethren. Formerly the monks publicly confessed faults committed against each other.

47

Today this idea is taken up in the confession of the mass, and in the kiss of peace, through which we express sorrow for our offences and pledge ourselves to live in peace with each other. It is this gesture that the Lord consecrates in the eucharist. After a further period of quiet reading and prayer another office is said. Called Tierce (the third hour of the day) it lasts only about ten minutes, and is an appeal to the Holy Spirit to come and bless the day ahead and its work.

The working day now begins, with all its activities, either in the farm, the workshops or the monastery itself. There is always work to be done there, in the kitchen, in the infirmary, in the guest house. At midday a short office again signals a pause in all these activities, before the monks take their main meal together.

Meals in the monastery are a community affair, and, in eating the same food and sitting together at a common table, the monk discovers again that he is truly one of many brethren. At first the clatter of cutlery and plates is all that can be heard, but soon comes the more pleasant sound of the reader's voice. Meals do not take place without some ritual. Although it might not seem so, these ceremonies are important for a community. Through them it acquires and preserves its own identity, and expresses something to itself about its life and ethos. Thus the meal is preceded by prayer. Then there is a moment of silence in which the gospel is read, and only after this do the monks turn their attention to the food.

After dinner is the time for siesta for those who want it. Others may read or occupy themselves in some other way. The office of None marks the resumption of work. At about 4.30 pm the bell signals the end of the working day. Those who can, come back to the church or the scriptorium, that is the room where the brethren come together for their *lectio*. Entering into this rhythm of peace in the evening, there is silence between the brethren, and this makes them more attentive to that light which shines without end.

It is this everlasting light* which they all praise at the office of Vespers before the evening meal. After the meal the Father Abbot

---

* On this theme of praising the Eternal Light see the beautiful Collect of Vespers for Monday of Week 3 of the psalter in the Roman Breviary

assembles the community and speaks to them—perhaps a conference on the *Rule of St Benedict* or on some other topic which will instruct and strengthen the community. Nothing then remains but to commit the night to the safe-keeping of the Lord and his holy Mother, the Queen of Heaven. This is done by the office of Compline and the singing of the *Salve Regina*.

The above outline of the monastic day is basically the same in any community. If a person wishes to experience the Cistercian life, he will normally be asked to live for a short period with the community, and will find the timetable corresponds closely to that given above.

## 3. *First steps in community*

The community is glad to have the newcomer in its midst, and he follows all its activities, from the workshops to the church, from the dormitory to the refectory. If the life is to form and motivate him, he must leave himself open to it from the beginning. Perhaps he will find some custom or practice incomprehensible or even slightly ridiculous. This does not matter. Nothing is there without good reason and it is only by living the Cistercian life that he will come to appreciate it. The monastic life itself is especially formative in the early stages of the growth of the young monk. In the very act of living the life many truths enter the spirit of the newcomer without his even being aware of them.

As well as the formation which the general rhythm of the life brings about, there is also a more intensive formation given the newcomers. They meet several times a day; they work together; and several times a week they come together for a meeting of the whole group with the Father Master who is especially responsible for them. This small group within the community provides the first apprenticeship in the common life. Each one is close to the others. No doubt he may well find some of their attitudes trying or their actions irksome. But he will also profit from them as he sees the generosity of their response to God or their joy in the life.

The influence of the Father Master is very considerable, and a number of elements, notably his nearness and availability, favour the establishment of a deep relationship with him. A set hour of dialogue with the Father Master each week is normal in most monasteries and to the extent that this is generously accepted the seeds of the monastic and spiritual life are sown in the heart of the novice. The novice can only say "Yes" to God by saying it to the community which he has joined. He thus opens himself to the community and its influence. He allows himself to be carried along by it and he gives himself to it generously. The formation he receives in this way cannot but become a source of new being and life for him.

The new arrival has cut himself off from the world through what is essentially a movement of love for God. His generous response brings him the feeling that God loves him. But this sentiment can in fact dim to the extent that the shock of leaving the world lessens. While the community's welcome for the newcomer will differ from one abbey to another, it will never be less than whole-hearted. The very fact of his coming confirms the monks in their vocation. Daily life together very quickly erodes any merely superficial fellowship. As the novice settles into the community he gets to know people better. The little weaknesses which at first he scarcely notices at all now become magnified; they annoy and prick his sensibilities; they can very quickly blur the fine picture of Cistercian life he had at the beginning.

The newcomer finds attitudes in the community which surprise him—for example a lack of warmth in the reception of guests or an individualism into which some of the brethren seem to have retreated. The very natural enthusiasm which made his first meetings with the community so pleasant abates, and his eyes are opened to the realities of daily life in the monastery. At the same time, the monks are trying to see if the novice is growing in the environment. They will have to decide whether or not to approve his joining them, and will give their opinion to the abbot or his Council before the novice is officially received into the community.

### 4. *From image to reality*
The novitiate, the time of formation par excellence, begins. The novice begins the new life by being clothed with the habit. Although

not given the long-sleeved robe of the monks called the cowl, he nonetheless truly enters the monastic life at this point. He gives himself completely to God in this life he has chosen, and even though there may be some slight disillusionment, this scarcely touches the profound conviction which has led him to the monastery. The gift which he has made of himself to the Lord is no doubt linked to a particular image of the monastic life. This image is formed by the way of life itself, by books on the subject, by the principles of monastic spirituality, by the rule, by the teaching of the great spiritual masters and writers, and by the wisdom of the first monks, the Desert Fathers.

However little the novice be open to theological questions or contemporary ideas, he will have to ask himself about openness to the world, about monastic hospitality, about witness and about the place of contemplatives in the Church. He will store up what he gleans from others about all these questions, and gradually from this and from his own resources he is formed. It is in himself that the strength of the formation process is to be found. The image he has of monastic life will motivate him to make that image a reality in his own life. And he will thus discover the wealth of generosity which is in him.

Perhaps he will conclude that he does not find the same generosity in the other monks! And his zeal may even lead him to say this to the community. He may speak of those faults and failings in the community which seem so obvious to him. This is grace for the novice, for he is now beginning to feel the burden of his brethren. They are showing him that they cannot be reduced to the image he has for them. So he himself must try to live up to the ideal of the life.

But God knows his times and his moments. The calm of the night does not long remain a peaceful invitation to prayer. It becomes oppressive, inviting the novice in a thousand ways to escape. All the activities of the day start to occupy his mind before their time with a demanding urgency. And there seems much to be said in favour of a return to his own room for a further short sleep. Surely he will be better able to meet the coming day after some extra rest? These suggestions do not come to him as idle insinuating thoughts but with a strength which will overpower him if he

51

hesitates at all. In this way he discovers the ambivalence of his own heart. He cannot see any sign of the determination and will which were so evident earlier. He discovers how little the night vigils attract him, though formerly he saw them as one of the most beautiful elements in the monk's life. Now they are only a nuisance. As for fasting—how strong his appetite and how tempting the dishes of the cook! He finds in himself no inclination to fast, no hunger for the eternal word which ought to displace his hunger for bread. Self-discipline does not come naturally to him.

The novice is discovering his own weakness. He cannot measure it, for it is beyond measure. If he could measure it he might take credit for it or find something in it to congratulate himself on. It is not something, it is nothing, an emptiness and a void within him. He feels his own limits and at the same moment the power of God. For it is when a man discovers himself that he discovers God, who although remaining always the Other, is more intimate to each man than man is to himself.

Other experiences too can open him to God. For instance a man of mature years may be set tasks that he considers demeaning or pointless. He may be carting manure in the garden and see no point in it. It will occur to him that with his talents he could improve the whole place, and could have someone else do this small service for him as part of the larger project. He should be in charge of such a scheme and not be wasting time as he is now!

Not to be given responsibility is a serious privation at an age when a man is at the peak of his strength and longs only to devote himself to a profession for the sake of a family. Instead of this, the novice finds himself apparently occupied by trivialities.

It may seem to him that this very positive element in the make-up of everyone is being denied him. But in fact it is to his benefit that it be denied him. God is asking for his trust. Jesus takes him into his hands, puts him in his care, says to him: "You are my responsibility, I will care for you". God reveals himself to him as a friend, or rather as one who longs for our friendship. He is no longer felt as distant and far away, but experienced as present and immediate, rich in love yet always poor in that he waits for our love.

## 5. *With God and the brethren*

The meeting with God is closely linked to the meeting with the brethren. This is the more true in a monastic community where the point of departure, the very reason for the meeting with each other, is avowedly in the domain of faith. If we analyse this we risk distorting it. If we abstract one element from it, we are in danger of losing sight of the other and both are essential. The community and the newcomer learn to know each other, and this takes place in an atmosphere of mutual trust. As the days go by the community gradually reveals itself and its inner life to the novice. What had been only surmised from the beginning is now seen clearly. At the same time the community recognises the novice as one of its own, and sees beyond the external behaviour and appearance to the interior depths, the heart given to God.

This mutual recognition is made concrete in very powerful fashion the day the novice promises obedience to his abbot according to the rule of St Benedict. He does this in the presence of all the assembled brothers. From this day he is vowed to God, tied by love to the Cistercian monastic life and to this community. From the viewpoint of canon law these first vows are temporary. In the time of St Benedict it was not so. The novice committed himself for life after one year in the monastery. This is no longer possible today. The aspirant must be allowed to leave the community at any time during the two or three years of probation.

However, we must ask whether a gift can be temporary, can be limited to one, two or three years. What we have here is not merely a preparation for something, nor is it merely a contract, it is an act of confidence in the call of God. This call is more or less clearly perceived already, and the young man is ready to give his life in answer to it. Therefore this first profession is fundamental. Solemn profession which juridically binds the monk until the end of his life will be no more than a renewal of this first offering. This solemn profession will be made in the clarity of a much greater interior light. The minimum delay of three years which must separate the first profession from it will have formed the young monk. The community will have called on him to perform various tasks, which are not indeed key posts in the monastery, but which mark a greater integration on his part into the community. For example he may have to help in the kitchen, in the laundry, in the tailor's shop, or perhaps he will be given responsibility for a workshop. In their own way these community duties are also a school of the Lord's service. By them the monk can serve the Lord in the brethren, who can be demanding and who are not always in good humour, and also in those brethren whose "Thank You" can warm his heart and give him back his joy in life. Life in community leads him to discover the many frailties of human nature. Things go wrong. We are hurt or offended. The only way to deal with this is to forget oneself and forgive, and continue to trust others despite everything. Up to now we have been talking about the relationship between the young monk and the community as a whole. A community is something more than the sum of the individuals in it. It has a life of its own and is greater than the people who make it up. Indeed it is a source of life and this would not be so if it were not composed of living people, who are themselves alive and vital. It is these who in hidden fashion keep a community alive.

As well as having a relationship with the community, the newcomer also has one with the Abbot and the Father Master. Friendship with these two can be of the greatest help to him in times of difficulty or doubt, when he is surrounded by darkness and temptation. Their desire is for his good, and they will offer him a shoulder to lean on, or an arm to support him. Because they are older, they know the sort of trials which come upon anyone who seeks to cultivate an interior life. They are therefore able to enlighten the young man and their counsel is objective and detached. Their lives are close to his and their paths often cross in the community. It is true of course that there is a considerable distance between the duties of the Abbot and the Father Master and those of the novice. But if he wants it, the conditions for a fruitful dialogue with these men exist.

The Abbot and the Father Master offer the young man their support and direction, and if necessary they will correct him, all in a spirit of true friendship. But they are not the only ones with whom he can have ties of real friendship. For friendships among the brethren are desirable. Such friendship is another stone in the building up of each one and of the whole community. It must not be exclusive, but rather open to all, and this demands great unselfishness and detachment.

If friendship between individuals is to develop in a closely-knit community, it must be marked by great discretion and sensitivity. Meetings for private conversation are possible, but the friendship will grow especially in the ordinary work of daily life, working together at the tasks given one in community. We must always remember that we have offered our lives to the Lord and this will dominate all our friendships. The many services which the community needs will provide opportunities for meeting. Each one will learn to appreciate the value of friendship through the affirmation his friends give him and their constant thoughtfulness. The monk can also have friends outside the community. Provided these are not possessive and exclusive, and that they do not withdraw the monk from his community, but rather confirm him in his vocation, then they are a blessing. They can be a breath of fresh air for the community.

Some of these relationships can be very strong and deep, but through them all the monk's vocation will grow in the heart of the community, on condition that the community is a living and vital centre of prayer. As in every vocation, the monk must strive for freedom. In order to follow Christ, he must try to free himself from himself, so that Christ may grow in him. Cistercian life has certain characteristics which are peculiar to itself. These are withdrawal from the world, liturgical prayer, continual supplication, the common life and stability in a place. These should be the characteristics of the one who enters this school. From the time of his formation he lives the same kind of monastic life that he will live for the rest of his life. Right from the beginning the life itself is one of the most powerful forces in his formation. He will make the Cistercian heritage his own, as he receives it from the hands of the living God in his community, and he in turn will pass it on. He will give thanks every day, never ceasing to wonder at the mercy of God and of the brethren*.

* Reference here is to the formula which the novice uses when asking for the monastic vows. He enters the Chapter Room and to the formal question of the abbot "What do you ask?", replies "The mercy of God and of the brothers".

# Chapter 4

## FOLLOWING CHRIST

### 1. *The workshop of prayer*

Since the twelfth century Cistercians have so built their monasteries that their purpose is clear—they are houses of God and places of prayer. You can see this in many of the medieval abbeys, such as Holy Cross in Ireland, the remains of Rievaulx in Yorkshire or Melrose in Scotland, or in the beautiful outline of the great Abbey of Tintern in Wales. The Cistercian spirit of simplicity is engraved to this day on the very stones.

Taste in decoration and building styles has changed down the centuries, but the order and arrangement of the monastic buildings has not. The workshop where God's work is done should be poor, sober and functional. The monk should aim at what is essential, rejecting comfort and anything superfluous, especially in decoration. Although it is true that the life style fashions the buildings and the site, it is also true that the buildings impose their own style on the life of the monks. A bare church does away with distractions and draws the attention to God alone. The careful blending of light and shade, the use of authentic materials, and an emphasis on sobriety of line will achieve this. Poverty demands neither bad taste nor ugliness.

Beauty and simplicity preserve the spirit from distraction and lead it to God. Beauty leads to contemplation and is a sort of sacrament of the eternal beauty of God. The monk's vision is purified in prayer. His outlook on the work is refined and transfigured. A man of prayer instinctively loves what is beautiful. Beauty is a language that speaks to him of what is beyond itself, and through it he comes to recognise the face of "the most beautiful of the children of men". Light falling into a forest clearing, the harmony of shapes, the play of colour, the mystery of the outline of a hand or a face, strikes his eye and leads him to go beyond appearances to a deeper reality. The sacred character of Holy Cross Abbey, for example, imposed itself on the builders who translated their perception of the world and of God into the material of the building. The ordinary laws of aesthetics were inadequate. Like an icon painter, they were trying to express the inexpressible. By stripping the church of everything that was sumptuous, they have somehow made present the transcendence of God. The heart of the monastery is the church, and it will normally face East, except where the lie of the land prevents this. The refectory, the community reading room, and the chapter room will be found on the four sides of the quadrangle called the cloister. Upstairs are the dormitory, the infirmary and the cells which communicate easily with the church. Other offices and places needed for the life of the community will be found in other parts of the house. Further away from this central area are the out-offices—the workshops, garages, farmyard and other buildings necessary for productive work, because like all men the monk earns his bread by the work of his hands. There will be a guest house for the reception of the monks' families and friends, and for retreatants. The cloister occupies a special place, to the point where in today's language this word is often used to designate the entire complex. Completely closed on its outer side, the cloister gets light through bays or windows which open on to an inner court we call the cloistergarth. It is the cloister which gives the buildings unity and cohesion. Life is organised around it. It communicates an atmosphere of recollection to the monk who quietly and slowly paces up and down here, ruminating on the Word of God*.

---

* In all this section the author is talking about a monastery built on the traditional lines, in a quadrangular pattern. In fact today this is no longer being done, and many modern monasteries all over the world are built either in "village" style with isolated blocks of buildings scattered over a campus, or as spokes of a wheel centring on a church, or with the work area at one side of the church and the living areas on the other. The variations are endless. The above would hold for the traditional medieval buildings which was the pattern followed up to about the year 1950.

## 2. *Far from the city*

The monastery is built in solitude. But this is not simply so that the monks may find peace and quiet there. They come here to do battle—the never-ending battle with evil that takes place in prayer. To the visitor however, the cloister does appear like a haven of peace, far from the world with its troubles and anxiety. Perhaps he sees there a reflection of the peace of God, inviting him to put aside the burden of care for a little while and refresh his soul, and so return to the noise and bustle of the city refreshed and renewed in the faith.

While this corner of solitude may be bathed in light and peace it is also the monk's battleground. Having left the world and come to the monastery, the monk finds the world again within, and especially within himself. The monastic community applies to itself what St Peter said to the first Christians: "Your enemy the devil, like a roaring lion, prowls around looking for someone to devour. Stand up to him firm in the faith, and remember that your brother Christians are going through the same kind of suffering while they are in the world" (1 Pet. 4:8). The monk in his solitude very quickly discovers a profound solidarity with his brothers in the city. He also faces a battle, and this is the struggle against the powers of egoism and pride, against the principles of division which exist in himself as well as in the community.

The monk is removed from many of the difficulties of life in the world, and indeed from many of its joys also—home and family, the social and political scene. But this is so only to allow him to concentrate his whole being, and all his strength on the warfare of the heart. He is like a competitor before an event, who withdraws from all occupations and goes into training.

Hidden in the bottom of a valley or isolated on a hilltop, the monastery is withdrawn from the world only in appearance. In reality it is enfolded in the world, not limited by its location to a particular place, but rather cast on the earth to touch the very heart-beat of creation. The way of life it offers is the Gospel in stark simplicity. The monastic life is the Christian life lived under conditions which favour the experience of God, as was clearly stated in the message sent by contemplative monks to the Synod of Bishops in 1967[8].

The solitary life which he has chosen turns the monk away from everything artificial and from concern with the superficial. While it is true that there is a distance between him and the society of men, this is not because he has fled from society. Indeed there is a sense in which, thanks to his detachment and distance from society, the monk is nearer to all men. He becomes the brother of all in a profound communion which does not have to manifest itself externally. As Evagrius of Pontus, one of the most celebrated of the Desert Fathers, said: "The monk is separated from all and united to all"[9]*.

Although he may seem to be free from the activity of building up the world, the monk is in fact deeply concerned with it. His choice of life brings him immediately to that place where the world must be brought to birth in the presence of God. He is inspired by that immense and ever-active yearning which runs through all creation, and strives to bring about the transformation of the Universe.

As the monks said in their message to the Synod in 1967:

> On the other hand, while the contemplative withdraws from the world, this does not mean that he deserts either it or his fellow-men. He remains wholly rooted in the earth on which he is born, whose riches he has inherited, whose cares and aspirations he has tried to make his own. He withdraws from it in order to place himself more intensely at the divine source from which the forces that drive the world onwards originate, and to understand in this light the great designs of mankind. For it is in the desert that the soul most often receives its deepest inspirations. It was in the desert that God fashioned his People. It was to the desert he brought his People back after their sin, in order to "allure her, and speak to her tenderly" (Hos. 2,14). It was in the desert, too, that the Lord Jesus, after he had overcome the devil, displayed all his power and foreshadowed the victory of his Passover.[10]

This is why the monastery is a kind of prophetic place, an antici-

* The quotation given here is from the translation of Evagrius made by Irénée Hausherr in *Les lecons d'un Contemplatif: Le traité d'oraison d'Evagre le Pontique* (Paris, 1968). The published English translation is by John Eudes Bamberger in *The Chapters on Prayer* and is slightly different. It runs "The monk is separated from all men and is in harmony with all".

pation of the world to come, a permanent declaration of a universe remade in God, a universe whose poles are charity and the praise of God.

## 3. *A school of love*

St Benedict offers his *Rule* to his disciples as a school of the Lord's service. It is not merely a collection of commandments and observances, it is a life. The counsels given by St Benedict are like milestones along the road which he himself has followed. His experience and the wisdom of everyday life have dictated them to him and gradually he set them down so that he could teach this life of faith to the disciples who came to him. He teaches conversion of heart, and the way to intimacy with God. His is a road of humility and love, a road that leads to rebirth in the Holy Spirit. It is a way that Jesus revealed to Nicodemus—"Do this and you will live".

The early Cistercians loved the image of a school. It appealed particularly to the men of the twelfth century which saw the rise of so many famous schools, the forerunners of our universities, such as Paris, Chartres and Oxford. The Cistercians opened a "School of Charity". Neither rhetoric, scholasticism nor profane science was to be learned there. The teaching was not done out of books. It was given in life and given abundantly. The teachers were not brilliant dialecticians but men who had met God and were experienced in his ways. They turned hearts to the word of God and taught the scholars the art of seeking God. To know oneself and to know God was all knowledge.

A man had to discover the misery of his own heart, caused by the wound of sin, so that it might be purified by contact with the loving heart of Jesus. The pupil in this school of love came to know by experience the great love with which the Father has loved him, and his own heart gradually became capable of the very charity of God. Under the influence of that divine pity which comes from the bosom of the Holy Trinity and embraces all men, he is gradually transformed in God.

## 4. *He humbled himself . . .*

"Go sell your possessions . . . and come follow me" (Mt 19:21).

We have seen how this word seized the heart of St Antony and changed his life. In some ways the same thing happens slowly and suddenly in the life of every man whom Jesus calls. Christ is the Way, the Truth and the Life. No one can come to the Father except through him (Jn 14:6). When Jesus calls, his presence is felt, his voice is heard, his love reaches out and touches the heart. A man already seized by the love of Christ is ready to follow him as a wife is ready to follow her husband. At this point the man we are talking about probably knows little of the reality of Christ's presence or of the way he must follow. But as he walks along the road, however painful it be, and however tempted he may be to give up, he will learn that it was truly Jesus who captivated him and is leading him out into the desert to comfort him (cf Hos. 2:14 ff). To commit oneself to follow Christ is not accomplished all at once. It takes a long time. Like life itself, it will evolve and gradually and imperceptibly be transformed as the years pass. Very often too, the reasons which led one to follow Christ change along the way. This is because love renews itself in showing itself, and it expands in sharing itself. Love is without measure.

To follow Jesus into the desert is to follow him in one aspect of his life, to reproduce a particular characteristic of his mission in oneself and one's own life, for the Church. The monk chooses to situate himself in the heart of that loving desire which draws the Son to the Father. He tries to make his own that unceasing murmur of the heart of Jesus — 'Abba, Father!''

He is thus led into the mutual love of Father and Son. He comes to the very heart of that mysterious dialogue between Jesus and his Father, which took place when the Lord went aside from men and spent the whole night in prayer: "Father, may your name be made holy, may your will be done" (Mt 6:10). The road the monk must follow is already traced out for him by Peter in his Epistle: "Christ suffered on your behalf, and thereby left you an example; it is for you to follow in his steps" (1 Pet 2:21). Jesus humbled himself and assumed our human condition that he might exalt it and through his obedience restore it to its former beauty. The monks of the Middle Ages had Christ's obedience constantly before their eyes. They meditated on it, they pondered it in their hearts so that

62

they might make it their own and live it. For was not Jesus himself the life and the truth?

In one of his sermons, St Bernard says:

> As for me, dear brothers, from the early days of my conversion, conscious of my grave lack of merits, I made sure to gather for myself this little bunch of myrrh and place it between my breasts. It was culled from all the anxious hours and bitter experiences of my Lord; first from the privations of his infancy, then from the hardships he endured in preaching, the fatigues of his journeys, the long watches in prayer, the temptations when he fasted, his tears of compassion, the heckling when he addressed the people, and finally the dangers from traitors in the brotherhood, the insults, the spitting, the blows, the mockery, the scorn, the nails and similar torments that are multiplied in the Gospels, like trees in the forest, and all for the salvation of our race. Among the teeming little branches of this perfumed myrrh I feel we must not forget the myrrh which he drank upon the cross and used for his anointing at his burial. In the first of these he took upon himself the bitterness of my sins, in the second he affirmed the future incorruption of my body. As long as I live I shall proclaim the memory of the abounding goodness contained in these events; throughout eternity I shall not forget these mercies, for in them I have found life.;[11]

If the monk truly follows Christ how can he fail to learn humility and obedience, so that his life and heart are gradually transformed? The way of humility is not easy. It is fraught with pitfalls. You are not necessarily humble by wanting to be so. Humility is not gained by willing it. We today are very conscious of counterfeit humility. Our acts of humility are subtle and ambiguous, and our efforts to take the last place can often lead us into untruth. Good will and good intentions alone will not buy humility. Only when the heart is touched by grace, and broken by the tenderness of God, will one be humble. Humility is the fruit of a meeting between a man wounded by sin and the loving mercy of God. The man whose eyes meet those of Jesus knows his own misery and sinfulness, and in that same moment he realises that he is forgiven. Confessing his sin he knows he is helpless, and this brings him to acknowledge the power and the love of God. Liberated and detached from himself, he depends solely on the power of God, and in his turn he becomes compassionate to all his brothers, as Jesus was. Recalling what marvels the Lord has done for him, he sees that everyone is enveloped in the love of God. Indeed it is in this love which God has for all people that the monk finds their true beauty and dignity.

In this way the monks of old led their disciples to a knowledge of themselves which is the first step in humility and the beginning of all conversion. When he has come this far the monk will look for work that is humble, he will want to be counted for nothing and will be at the service of all. He will wish to pass unseen, for God is everything to him. His behaviour and his gestures will reveal the state of his heart. This is the state St Benedict spoke of when he described the summit of the degrees of humility. "Everything which formerly he observed only with difficulty, he now begins to do without any labour, as it were naturally and by habit for the love of Christ" (RB 7:68).

## 5. *The labour of obedience* (RB Prol. 2)

Jesus' desire to do his Father's will led him to obedience, obedience even unto death on the cross. As a disciple of Christ who came not to do his own will but the will of him who sent him, the monk professes obedience. This way of obedience is held in suspicion today. Here again, as in the case of humility, it is in the Easter grace of Jesus that we must situate obedience if we are to understand it, and to recognise its truth and richness. In order to follow Jesus in his obedience, we must take the risk of dying to ourselves, and immersing ourselves in the mystery of Christ's death and resurrection.

Obedience is not a matter of carrying out orders willy-nilly, nor of doing merely what the superior commands. It goes much deeper than that. To obey is to commit oneself to the state of being a servant as Christ was, and thus to make a total offering of oneself. The whole monastic tradition cannot be wrong when it says that obedience must be offered not only to the abbot, but also to the brethren. "Obedience . . . is to be shown by all, not only to the abbot, but also to one another as brothers" (RB 71:1). Obedience is not given merely to hierarchical superiors, but is an attitude of soul which spontaneously expresses itself to everyone whom the monk meets. It implies that we are willing to put our own desires aside, even so far as to prefer another's wishes.

If we are to understand this obedience, we must look at the obedience of Jesus. Far from claiming his right to be equal to God, Jesus took on the form of a slave, and came to do the will of his Father (Ph. 2:6-7). He submitted his will and his own desires to the will of the Father, to the point that he had no will except the Father's. It is difficult for us to understand this communion between Father and Son. Possibly we understand better that pairing which is master/slave, exploiter/exploited. If we think this way we end up thinking of God as a tyrant. Between Jesus and his Father there is only the logic of love. The Father's will is neither caprice nor domination, but the desire of love, the design of redemption, the very heart of mercy . . . it is tenderness itself. Far from crushing or destroying the self, the obedience of Jesus is a communion, an adherence to and a sharing in that same desire, the love of the Father's will. The Father and the Son recognise and desire each other in a single movement. This embrace which unites them St Bernard calls "the kiss of the mouth". If Jesus has given up his body, soul and spirit, this is because the greatest joy and the greatest freedom possible is to be united to the one who is our heart's desire.

Jesus broke for ever the bonds which chained master and slave. He breached that vicious circle where the victim became the executioner, and the exploited the exploiter. In this lies the revolutionary character of the New Commandment. Jesus inaugurated a new way of life and he showed how we must live in the Kingdom. He who was formerly the victim pardons his executioner and calls him brother. The slave loves his master and forgives him, so that the master now reconciled kneels before him. The enemy come to attack receives the embrace of friendship. "If there is this love among you", says Jesus, "then all will know that you are my disciples" (Jn 13:35). This strategy of love replaces all other struggles, all other conflicts in the New Testament. With it everything is possible. When he delivers himself into the hands of another man and undertakes to live with his brothers, the monk in fact abandons himself to God. Like Jesus he has no other place in which to exercise this obedience to the Father than in the daily grind, the commonplace task, the burden of the common life and in the ordinary routine of the day. He does this to give witness to the new world, the world of fraternal love, the language of which is mutual obedience. The monk does not have to wait for an order to be given before he obeys*. Much more profound and demanding, his commitment rather puts him instead in a ceaseless condition of obedience. The monk is in a *state* of obedience as we speak of a *state* of grace. All relationships and all situations are approached in this same state of soul. An interior attitude, a paradoxical liberty, enables him to apprehend what is real, and welcome each brother and his needs with good will. Right through the day, he discovers a thousand occasions for giving way to another's wish, for listening to or accepting his brother's advice, so he may know the truth which his brother has, and try to resolve the differences between them. In the ordinary works and services of the monastery he will carry out his task without seeking to impose either his own methods or his own opinions. He will prefer to stick to the project as it is being done by his brothers.

Perhaps one day he may find that he has to obey more deeply, or acquiesce more crucially in the desire of another. St Benedict speaks of obedience in impossible things (RB 68). This might be a bizarre order from a superior, a lack of understanding on the part of the brethren, or giving up some work which he had begun. Whatever it be, there will always be question of following Jesus where one does not wish to go (cf Jn 21:18).

In the eyes of many such obedience may seem to be servile submission or an abuse of authority. The eyes of faith discern another will in the command, even though it be capricious, or erroneous, or unjust. "You would not have power over me unless you were given it from above" (Jn 19:11). The monk uses the occasion to enter into the will of the Father. In an extreme case he can appear to be crushed. But in fact by inserting another dimension and another design into the situation he is the one who overcomes. Even though troubled he remains faithful, and thus achieves slowly

* It must be noted that a monk can always make representations about any order he is given (cf RB Chapter 68).

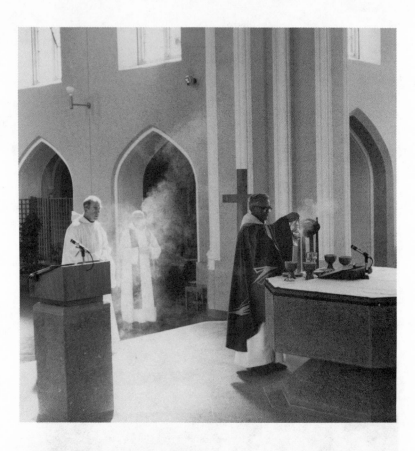

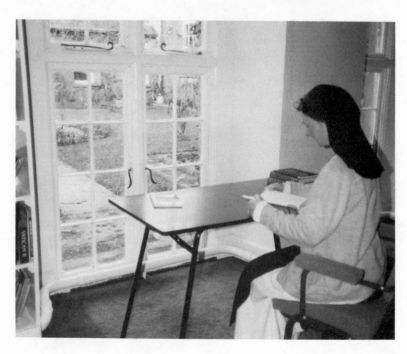

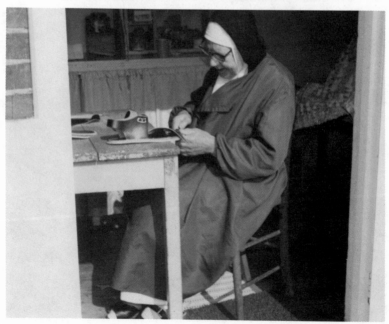

and without fanfare the immense liberty of being able to say: "Father not my will but thine be done ..." (Mt. 26:39).

In this way the labour of obedience heals a man who has been wounded and divided by his will for power. Obedience is a school of charity which corrects the curvature of the soul which has turned back on itself. It is the workshop where the Holy Spirit works to disengage the very depths of our heart from false needs and deceptive securities, and to open a passage for the breath of life, the desire of God.

Following Christ in humility and obedience is real work, a "labour" as St Benedict calls it. It is an intense struggle in which the monk will feel that he is expending all his strength and being hampered by his limitations. The first generous impulse which carried him along at the beginning quickly subsides, and he learns what it costs to deliver himself up to this burnishing of the Holy Spirit. Just when the monk appears vanquished in this struggle between unequal forces, the Holy Spirit himself takes over and becomes the motive force within him, the dynamism of future progress. This is the object of the combat which we call asceticism.

The monk, wounded and vanquished, has no other resource but to abandon himself to the power of the Spirit, who thereafter carries on this work, and leads him to rest in God. The monk must learn not to put his trust in his own resources. He must depend on God alone. Through this abandonment of obedience, the Holy Spirit brings about this work of God in him.

## 6. *An older brother*

For this work to succeed, the young monk needs the help of a senior or a spiritual father. It does not matter what we call him. What we mean is a monk experienced in the ways of God, skilful in winning souls (RB 58:6), and able to open them to the action of the Holy Spirit. This latter phrase is very exact, because our hearts must be opened to allow the source of life within them to spring up. Just as the nutshell must be opened if the kernel of the almond is to be got out, the soul must be opened if the Spirit within is to be freed for life.

In an atmosphere of faith and trust, the monk tells this senior about his doubts and temptations, his problems, his faults and mistakes, his joys and what God has done for him. He looks for counsel, encouragement and strength. He asks the senior to discern the work of the Holy Spirit, and to distinguish the voice of God from the babble of thoughts and desires which crowd in upon him. His question is: "What must I do to have life?"

Filled with the same faith, the senior receives the monk who comes to him as a grace. Reflecting the mercy of God he welcomes this brother in his weakness, and in humility and prayerfulness he listens to what the Spirit is saying to him. While he must make the brother docile to the voice of the Spirit, he must also efface himself in order to be a simple bearer of the word of this same Spirit. Through all trials of whatever kind, the vexations of common life, the inevitable confrontations, he patiently leads the disciple to a knowledge of his own limitations. He helps him discover his faults and accept them as true riches. He accompanies him in the discovery of his interior world, of alternating light and shadow. In such a climate of true friendship no desire is repulsed. On the contrary the senior receives him with respect and love, no matter what his condition or state. Whatever is good in the disciple deserves to be honoured, whatever is disordered he will restore. Sometimes this can be done as easily as welcoming him; at other times it will need patience and discernment. In this way the young monk is gradually initiated into what used to be called the discernment of spirits. He learns to distinguish between what favours liberty of spirit and what risks reducing it. The older monk like a patient physician recreates the harmony and unity which should exist in this man whose psychological heritage is to some extent marred and faulty, but who is also the bearer of a spiritual life of which he is scarcely aware, and will one day become the living centre of his being. He walks beside him in the spiritual struggle, and he will always welcome him when he has been wounded in this struggle. The monk confesses his weakness and once more puts himself under God's loving care to be filled with the power of the Holy Spirit. Thus freed from all masks and defences, the young man will come to love himself truly, and he will also discover true love of his neighbour. Beyond the troubles and turbulence of life he will come to an interior joy, to a repose and peace without end. Very gradually, in the course of this dialogue, the senior will truly bring forth the novice to the spiritual life in fulfilment of the word of Jesus inviting us to be reborn from on high (Jn 3:7).

As the ear of his heart becomes attuned to the Word of God, the disciple will find himself capable of hearing the call of the Spirit, and of seeing the presence of Christ in events. Then he will be docile to that mysterious voice which murmurs within: "Come to the Father"[12].

# Chapter 5

## A HEART PURIFIED BY THE WORD OF GOD

The fundamental activity of the monk, which in the end tends to become his only activity, is prayer. This prayer is nourished by the Word of God, which is generously provided by the monastic life. But if the word of God is to bear fruit in the monk and to become prayer, he must dwell in the depths of that place which is given him where he can hear and welcome the word—he must return to his own heart.

### 1. *Return to your heart*

The advice the ancient fathers unceasingly gave to the novice was this: "Return to your own heart". What does this mean? The young monk soon realises how difficult it is to approach God to enter into contact with him. We have already described the first often unavailing steps which help him deepen his inner life. An important aspect of this maturing process is the discovery, perhaps at first only the presentiment, of an inner organ which will allow him enter into contact with God. What is it that we pray to God with? What faculty do we use in order to pray? Do I use my intelligence, do I reflect on my concept of God, trying to deepen this and compare it with other realities that I already know? Perhaps I can to some extent deduce some conclusions from this, for example that God is all-powerful, God knows everything, God is the ultimate reason for my being, God is my creator.

These ideas are useful, but they can lead me to think that in this way I can come to a full knowledge of God. In fact they remain superficial and can end by wearying me. They are always open to very plausible counterarguments, which can sometimes shake my perhaps painfully-acquired convictions. I must also ask if such reasoning can really satisfy my deep thirst for God. Does reasoning of this kind truly put me in touch with God? The answer, I think, is "No".

I can of course turn to my imagination. I can try to represent God to myself using images which are familiar to me. However, even these images — and they are holy for they are used by the Church in the liturgy — cannot speak to me interiorly except to the extent that my heart has been made truly receptive to their spiritual depth. There is always a certain danger with feelings in religion. Are they not artificial? How can I stir up repentance, sorrow or love again in my heart unless God himself intervene and lead to them again, buried as they are in the deepest part of myself, in this place he wishes to reveal to me?

The Bible gives this interior place the name "heart". The best description of the heart in this sense is given by some Fathers of the church who designate it as "the place of God in us". There is a place in every man where God touches him and where he himself is constantly in contact with God. This is simply because at every instant God holds us in being. Ceaselessly we come forth from his hands. The place where this creative contact with God takes place is deep within me. If I can reach it I can touch God. If I can arrive at a point where I can free myself from every other reality and bring the gaze of my spirit to bear on this point exclusively, I can meet God.

Some of the mystics have spoken of this place as an abyss or a well whose dizzying depths draw us like a magnet. Are we not in fact continually haunted by this desire for God, which leads us insensibly towards that reality in ourselves which is both the deepest and the most divine part of our being? Other spiritual writers have taken their imagery from height, while others again speak of the pinnacle of the spirit or the fine point of the soul. They invite us to ascend these heights where we will meet God. This place is therefore the most precious centre of our being. There we come forth from the hand of God as his creatures; there we are begotten as his children.

If we are to understand this mystery we must first of all believe what the gospels say about the divine persons in God. The eternal birth of the Word, in which we share by grace, goes on endlessly at this innermost centre of our being. It is like an efficacious and powerful echo of the divine. The more I try to recollect myself around these springs of eternity that open wide within me, the more I try to lose myself in these depths, the nearer I come to the divine life which flows out from them. The more too can I hope to be seized by Christ who dwells there, to be swept up by the Spirit of God who gives me life in secret. Since I already draw all my being from the bosom of the Father, I can hope that the Spirit will in fact lead me into the very life of the Trinity.

That place where God dwells in me is also the place of prayer. Long before I am aware of it or before I take an interest in it, this prayer is going on ceaselessly within me. In effect, it is not I who give myself to prayer, but the Holy Spirit who never ceases to pray in me with inarticulate groans, as St Paul says in his letter to the Romans (cf Rom. 8:26). This prayer is my heart's treasure. It is a hidden treasure which is buried in the deepest part of my being, access to which is presently obstructed by a host of realities which distract me from prayer. These tend to keep me at a superficial level of my being. Until my heart is truly detached I cannot cope with these temptations without losing contact with the fire smouldering within me.

It is important to insist on this: right from the beginning, prayer has already begun before I do anything — it comes before any of my efforts and techniques. From the moment when I received the life of God in baptism, prayer has been poured into my heart along with the Holy Spirit who was then given to me (Rom 5:5). Prayer is there; it abides there. The Holy Spirit in person intercedes there for me and for all the saints. It is he who celebrates an unceasing liturgy, who makes the voice of Christ my voice, who lifts me up before God, and who, even when I do not know it, captivates the heart of God on behalf of the Church, the world and that sinner who I am. "To live in a state of grace" means that at a deep level I live in a state of prayer. At the beginning this prayer is entirely unconscious so all my efforts will consist in letting the prayer flow out and spill over into my consciousness. Nothing more than that. From being unconscious, this prayer must become conscious. I must

73

allow it take me over from within, so that I can become united with it, and take direction of it, while allowing myself to be borne up by it. The monastic life has no other objective than to awaken the heart and make it aware of that prayer which is always going on within it.

## 2. *Lectio divina*

From what we have said, we can see the vital role played by the Word of God in the life of the monk. This is why St Benedict in the very opening words of the *Rule* insists on the importance of a humble listening attitude: "Listen carefully, my son, to the master's instructions, and attend to them with the ear of your heart. This is advice from a father who loves you; welcome it, and faithfully put it into practice" (RB Prol. 1).

While it is true that it is within ourselves that God will come to meet us, it is also true that his coming will be sparked off by something outside ourselves. What is within awakes at the call of something from without. This can be an event, or it can be our brethren, our hopes or our disappointments, friendship or solitude, temptation or even sin. All these are shot through with the light of the word of God. Sometimes indeed a trial does not yield up its meaning without the grace of a creative light of the word of God. Sorrows are a sort of rebirth. In them my being at its deepest level, and my heart living in the presence of God, are brought to birth. This is because the Word has created me. It keeps me in being. By it I am ceaselessly reborn. It accompanies me all during this earthly life. It clears the way ahead of me. It shows me the path. It is a lamp for my steps and a light for my path, as the psalm says (Ps. 118). Every day the monk devotes a certain length of time to *lectio divina*. The use of this Latin term is not due to any attempt on the part of monks to preserve their own jargon. They retain this Latin phrase because it expresses something specific which tends to get lost in translation into a modern language. *Lectio divina* means "divine reading". At first sight that idea may seem simple, but in fact it is both deep and rich. The adjective *divina* shows that we are not dealing here with any kind of reading. Certainly it is not profane reading; it provides neither erudition nor mere amusement. But it is also something more than what might be called pious or edifying reading. It is even more than spiritual reading, in the sense in which this phrase is used today. It is called divine because in it God gives us his Word directly. It is not a matter of reading things about God; God takes the initiative and intervenes in person. In *lectio divina* God speaks to and addresses each person individually, and the reader must give himself as best he can to the Word of God. This idea cannot be expressed any better than by the phrase *lectio divina*.

Furthermore, the monk is not only a reader. He is also, and even more so, a listener. He listens to what comes to his ears, especially to the ears of his heart. The word *lectio* originally designated reading proclaimed in public and therefore *listened to*. "To read" meant to read aloud in a way that could be heard by the whole assembly. It is only afterwards, even among monks, that it meant reading to oneself in silence.

In one sense *lectio* provides a structure for the monk's day. He is called to it from the time he rises until he retires, and even at night the Word of God is read to him. As soon as he assembles with the community, the reading begins. No sooner does he retire than he thinks again on the word of St Jerome: "Let sleep find you with your pen in your hand and the holy page itself receive your head which falls upon it"[13].

The Word comes to the monk in the Office, of which indeed it is the very heart. The readings at Vigils are long. The two great offices of morning and evening, Lauds and Vespers, likewise have lengthy readings. During the little hours the readings are shorter, sometimes only a few verses, but they are to the point. These hours mark the rhythm of the day, calling the monk from his work and cares to recollection and interior listening. But *lectio* does not end with the office, with that long moment of silence when the whole community is united in the Lord, having heard his word. It continues in the silence of the cell or the recollection of the cloister. The time before dawn, between Vigils and Lauds, is particularly good for *lectio divina* in private. The heart is then free of all the preoccupations which press upon it during the day. During part of the year, it is still night. In summer one can be present at the slow rising of the sun, the bright light gradually chasing away the shadows of night. Did not St Peter compare the word of God to a "lamp shining in a murky place, until the day breaks and the morning star rises to illuminate your minds"? (2 Pet. 1:19).

*Lectio* goes on all through the day, even though work obliges the monk to close the book and give his attention to something else. The monks of old knew large sections of the Scriptures by heart, notably the psalms and the gospels. Thus their rumination on the word of God could continue despite their occupations. The word was not simply listened to—it tended to become prayer, uninterrupted prayer, as it were breathed out by a heart that was itself prayer. But how do you practise *lectio* so that the heart itself becomes prayer?

## 3. *The Word awakens the heart*

To talk about either a method or a technique would not be correct. These words imply the effort of someone to attain a foreseen result, to reach an objective which has been planned for. Now the effort we are talking about here does not really belong to man, nor does the result depend on him. The power at work in *lectio*, as in prayer, belongs exclusively to the word of God. So also does its fruit, the new being which the word of God and prayer produce.

The word of God looks like a human word, but the power that animates it belongs to God alone. "The word which comes from my mouth shall prevail; it shall not return to me fruitless without accomplishing my purpose, or succeeding in the task I have given it" (Is 55:11).

The word of God can create all things anew in the hearer whom it touches. It strikes and it wounds, but it does so to reawaken, to cure, to heal and to restore. It strikes the heart especially, for the heart is its special domain. The heart is the only organ by which a man can hear the word of God for what it really is—the word of GOD.

Man's heart, as we have already said, is the place of God. If we want to hear the word of God we must listen with our heart. We must make *it* the place where the word is heard. We must learn to read with our heart and this in itself is a discipline and an asceticism. It is indeed one of the fundamental disciplines of the monastic life and is akin to the interior place of prayer spoken of at the beginning of this chapter.

The activity of our reason, our imagination or our superficial sensibility are not in themselves sufficient to attain this. They will not enable us to hear the word of God. At a given moment a great withdrawal of these faculties must take place, a sort of fast must be imposed on them.

We do not wish to imply by this that scientific or exegetical study of the Bible is useless or contrary to prayer. Not at all. A better knowledge of the word of God and its history will certainly help us understand more clearly what this word is saying to us today. But such knowledge is only a preparatory stage in that process whereby God infallibly brings about the coming of his word. This word must be made new every day for the believing reader.

There comes a time therefore, when the monk will close the commentaries and put aside the dictionaries and concordances. He will no longer ask questions or pose problems. Nor will he run after representations of the word in his imagination, nor lean on the feelings which these can arouse. He will try instead to rest before God in reverent and loving attention, while his interior faculties remain empty.

He must work to create this emptiness, this space within, so that the power of God's word can fill it. Only then will this power spring up like a flash of light or as a force which can transform me. This does not normally happen quickly. Perseverance, humility and patience are needed, and not some sort of interior searching and questioning which would be no help at all. What the monk must do is nurture his desire for the word of God in faith and trust.

The attitude of soul and heart which we are here describing is not always either easy or comfortable. The reason for this is that it is an attempt to persevere in what is in fact an interior desert. This is especially so if the word of the Bible has not yet become alive and life-giving for the monk. He does not know where to turn. He has no interior point of reference other than a gentle awareness that has come to him from the Holy Spirit. He is tempted to take again the well-trodden paths of the old certainties that he knows. He wants the solid historical commentary, which will enlighten his intellect, or the pious meditation which will warm his heart, once more. He must resist these desires when he applies himself to *lectio divina*. He must patiently persist in his attempts, putting all his hope in the power of God who is present in his word, and in the love of God who wishes to speak to him at this moment.

In general however, the beginner in *lectio* does not have to wait too long. Suddenly a word will light up. He will be touched interiorly. Perhaps he will be seized by a powerful emotion. He may feel himself overcome by the power of the word of God. He will lose himself in it easily. Sometimes tears will come without effort on his part. They are the fruit of grace. Such an experience is important in the life of any believer especially the first time it happens. The heart feels as though it has been wounded by the sword of the word of God. "The word of God is alive and active, sharper than any two-edged sword. It cuts through to where the soul and spirit meet, to where joints and marrow come together. It judges the desires and thoughts of men's hearts" (Heb. 4:12).

Our heart is the place of God. God is there and we do not know it. Our heart sleeps and only the word of God can waken it. This word comes to bring it life, and filled with this life the heart stirs and awakens. The power of God which is in his word strikes it and makes it vibrate with and echo to the very life of God. The word seeks out our heart and then our heart seizes on the word of God. The two recognise each other. In this first blinding by the word of God, our heart truly hears the word and in that same instant recognises itself as a new being, recreated before God in the very power of his word. Henceforth things will never be the same. A new doorway has been opened. A crucial threshold has been crossed. A new criterion of discernment has been given to us. Having once recognised God's power in his word, so unlike all other inward experiences, we can recognise it again when it comes to us, just as we can thereafter detect its absence.

The first meeting with the word is comparable to the first profound spiritual experience of our lives. It is part of our very being, not just something pious or moving in the memory, but something truly life-giving for the whole of our spiritual lives.

Such a blinding flash by the word of God does not ordinarily last very long. St Bernard noted this when he said: "The hour is short, the time is brief". But the short duration does not matter, for in some way the experience is outside time, because it has something of eternity about it. Yet it can diminish or even disappear. Its memory will remain however, and this memory will haunt us. It will burn in our heart and nourish a desire which can feed our hunger for *lectio* for a long time to come. The memory can itself become a secret hunger like a new and hidden presence, which draws us to God in all we do though we may not be consciously aware of it. But God may allow the memory of this sweetness, or anyhow the sensible awareness of it, to disappear. Then in prayer and in reading we are once more face to face with darkness. This time, however, we are able to deal with it. We have been up against it before, and we now know by experience what the strength and the light of the word of God really mean. We understand how they can spring up despite all the obstacles which we more or less unconsciously put in their way. God saved us from darkness once. His light pierced through it. If he now leads us in a new way and along an unknown road, he will without doubt make his light shine out again in a more striking and powerful fashion. Our only attitude must be one of patient love and trust.

Mentioning this attitude leads us, before we go on to develop our account of monastic prayer, to say something about the asceticism of the monk. For this ascetical discipline is closely linked with the search for God and hence we must treat of it, however briefly.

# Chapter 6

## ASCETICISM — AN EXERCISE IN GRACE

### 1. *The meaning of asceticism*

The word asceticism is not much in favour nowadays, even among spiritual writers, despite the fact that it was once one of the key formulae of all spiritual literature. No doubt the present situation is due to a misunderstanding. As we have already seen, the original meaning of the word was simply an exercise or training. The spiritual life does not grow and develop in a vacuum. Certain conditions and a particular way of acting are needed if it is to evolve and intensify. It would be a mistake however to think that if we do certain things or carry out certain actions, this will happen. The interior life grows through grace. All progress in the spirit is a matter of exercising oneself, not in one's own ascetical prowess but in the freely given grace of Christ. Hence we have called this chapter "an exercise in grace", for this is the essence of all ascetic effort. During the first centuries of monastic life, everyone accepted without question the need for asceticism. Monasteries were not more ascetical or less ascetical, more penitential or less penitential. Each lived its life in the situation it found in the place, according to local customs and needs, but all accepted that asceticism is integral to monastic life. Later, with the rise of reform movements, new stress was put on the ascetical side of the life, in protest against an obvious relaxation. In this sense the Cistercian way, being part of a reform movement, has always been particularly marked by the serious attention it gives to asceticism.

The classic ascetical practices, common to all monastic life, are well-known. These are obedience, celibacy, holding our goods in common, vigils and fasting. Each of these engages the body in a type of behaviour which is never that to which a person is naturally drawn. Restrictions often involving total abstinence are imposed.

Their aim is not to reduce anything in man (although it may look like that at first sight) but to promote another part of him, a better part which cannot be brought to light except by renunciation.

It is right and normal that the body should be part of the spiritual adventure to which man is called. Man's spirit does not exist apart from or outside his body, at least in this life. His body is an integral part of his being. He needs his body to express his life and this holds for even the most profound and spiritual aspects of that life. If he is to come to grips with true spiritual growth he needs his body just as much as he needs his spiritual faculties. A genuine interior life can grow only through the body. This is true of every system of spiritual development inside or outside the Christian religion. We might also remark that the main forms of the ascetical life are common to all the great religions.

But the integration of the body into the way of spiritual development is even more necessary for the Christian than for others. The body as well as the spirit is marked by that congenital weakness which Scripture calls sin. Baptism has made us radically holy but it has not removed all the consequences of sin. The seeds of sin have remained in our bodies—which are one with our souls—and constitute a sort of hidden bent or inclination to evil in us. Therefore grace must confront sin in the body. The Christian life becomes a gradual taking over of the body by grace. Grace puts sin to death in the body, that is to say it mortifies the body in the most fruitful sense in order to make it capable of being transfigured. All mortification (and this is only another word for asceticism) ought to lead to this transfiguration. In this way asceticism is rather like death. Death is only a preliminary for the Christian but it is indispensable to the resurrection of the new life in Jesus Christ.

## 2. Death and resurrection

In speaking of asceticism, we cannot evade this fundamental expression—death and resurrection in Jesus Christ. Asceticism is simply our sharing in the paschal mystery of Jesus, the mystery of his death and rising to the new life in God. Asceticism aims to bring this sharing to its fulness, even before our death. Every step on the way of asceticism takes us deeper into this mystery and allows its power to cut a path for us through life. Our body is gradually transformed into Christ's image and likeness and this is done by means of mortification. In order to bring about our salvation, Jesus has taken a body to himself. He has become incarnate in this world of ours to confront the forces of sin and triumph over them in his life and in his death. It is in the flesh, says St Paul, that Jesus has triumphed over sin (Eph. 2:14). Following the example of Jesus we also must put sin to death in our bodies, and thus the power of Christ's life, given to us in baptism, will triumph. Every ascetical practice brings us into the mystery of Christ, and enables us to make progress in a very specific way in the life of Jesus, which should be manifest in us. In this sense every ascetical practice has an efficacy proper to itself.

It is true that all ascetical effort aims at bringing about the growth of the life of Christ in us, and this takes place in the deepest part of our being. But each individual practice is concerned with a particular area of that life, and this is important. Every ascetical sign possesses an efficacy which is proper to it, and which in a sense is naturally inherent in it. Thus we can speak of an asceticism which is natural to man and makes him fully human. For example interior and exterior silence joined to solitude naturally favour recollection, and enable a man to concentrate on his interior world. It is also evident that the hours of the night are more propitious to quiet and peaceful meditation, and that fasting causes a hunger for spiritual things, and that celibacy creates an affective void within, which calls for fulfilment by profound and more universal love.

There exists a natural mysticism, the techniques of which are not all that different from those used by Christian monks. Those who engage in it testify to an interior wholeness which we do not always see in the life of the Christian. In so far as technique or the perfection of a particular means is concerned, the natural mystics can often teach the believer something and help him in his search.

However we must say clearly that such asceticism, despite some good results, is not what Jesus Christ is seeking from his disciples. Only that ascetic effort which is the fruit of grace will truly promote the life of the Holy Spirit in their hearts. There is a fundamental disparity between all human effort, however perfect it be, and the gift of grace which is given us in Jesus Christ. Grace is always gratuitous. This is the fundamental fact of all Christian experience, and this is eminently true of mysticism. Without the gift of grace it is not Christian at all, but either pagan or simply a pastiche of ethics. God does not give himself according to the measure of our efforts. Jesus has not come for virtuous people but for sinners (Lk 5:32). He does not want what we call our virtues. He seeks our weakness so that his strength may grow in us without any limit as St Paul tells the Corinthians (2 Cor 12:9).

All ascetical effort therefore must be rooted in Jesus Christ. It must follow his example and imitate his life. The forms of asceticism which monks have spontaneously used down the centuries are those which Christ used at one time or another during his earthly life.

He was perfectly obedient in all things even unto death. The author of the Epistle to the Hebrews goes so far as to say that his body was given him in view of obedience (Heb. 10:5-9). He always lived as a celibate. He did not have any place where he could lay down his head (Lk. 9:58). He undertook periods of intense fasting (Lk. 4:2). He frequently retired into a desert place to spend the whole night in prayer (Mk 1:35; Lk. 6:12).

The ascetical programme of the monk draws all its force from the power that Jesus placed in these very exercises by practising them during his earthly life. It is by contemplating Jesus that the monk is able to re-create them in his own life. The ascetical exercises of the monk are the very ascetical exercises of Christ himself. And the monk's power to do them was won for him by Christ, when he used these same practices in his own life to meet real temptations and trials and to overcome them once and for all.

The other point we must make is this. If any ascetical effort is to become truly Christian, it must be emptied of all its human power and potential and brought even to the point of failure, so that it can be taken over by the power of Christ. It is in our weakness and emptiness that the power of Christ is most active. Any asceticism that is truly evangelical is an asceticism of weakness and of poverty.

## 3. *An asceticism of weakness*
The aim of all ascetic effort is to make oneself nothing, after the

example of Jesus Christ, described by St Paul in his letter to the Philippians: "Divine nature was his from the first, but he did not think to snatch at equality with God; but made himself nothing, assuming the nature of a slave" (Ph. 2:6). This nothingness is the closest we can come to God. It is a dying to self so as to be fully open to God. Our selfishness is *the* obstacle to God's life and the action of his Spirit within us.

By a strange paradox, the ascetic effort itself must share in this dying, this making ourselves to be nothing. It cannot achieve its goal of itself. At the precise point where our efforts fail, the power of God intervenes in order to bring our efforts to a perfection which we cannot reach by our own power.

We are not talking here about some physical effort as though the ascetic could push his body as far as human capacity could go. We are talking about a moral nothingness, a self-effacement which is the bitter realisation that the ascetical effort surpasses our strength and that God does not respond automatically as we had expected. God's grace is not to be measured by human effort.

This state of nothingness, this recognition of our own inadequacy, was called "*acedia*" by the ancient fathers. Known in English as "accidie", it is *the* place of temptation for the monk. There he comes up against his own weakness and inadequacy and can even come up against despair. He can turn against himself or against God. It seems that this really is a decisive moment in spiritual development, and that in it a man is brought face to face with his own depths. Each of us has a psychological make-up that is vulnerable and that can disintegrate. It is to be expected that so powerful a trial as this, which calls all our habitual ways of acting into question, would bring us to the very depths of our weakness. It is in these habitual ways of acting that we find our reassurance and security. Accidie forces us to re-examine and question not only our relationship with others, but with God himself. We find that we must re-examine the way we act towards God and how we understand him. It is precisely at this point that God intervenes. He comes to save us when we are weakest.

We would like to cite here one of the most ancient documents of Egyptian monasticism, the letter of Macarius. This is one of the best explanations of how the ascetical effort of the monk has no other aim than this radical stripping of self that we have been talking about. It is possible that at the beginning of monastic life the discipline of asceticism seems easy. Quite soon, however, this discipline and the effort it demands can seem absolutely beyond the capacity of the monk.

According to Macarius, when God sees that the monastic life with its early consolations pleases the beginner, he puts him to the test. This is done to see if he will truly renounce these joys and resist the prince of this world. Thus the monk finds he cannot fast. He is on the point of being overcome by the weakness of the body or the heaviness of time which never passes. Time seems endless. Temptation presses upon him. He wonders how long he can go on with his work. He wonders will God pardon his sins. Temptations to unchastity crowd in upon him. He feels that he is weak and wonders if he can support the burden of chastity at all. All these temptations stress that life is long, that virtue is difficult, and that its weight is heavy and insupportable. He feels his body weak and his nature fragile[14].

This is a sort of first wave of temptation, after which God gives some respite. This enables the monk to renew his strength to hold out against the enemy. But the respite is short and the assault inevitably comes again:

> When the good God sees that the heart of the monk prevails against the enemy, he gradually withdraws from him the strength which sustains him, and he allows the enemy to attack him by different temptations—of the flesh, of pride and of vainglory. This happens to such an extent that he is like a ship without a helmsman which is driving on the rocks. His heart withers and fails within him. God allows him to be as it were taken by each of these temptations. . . . In this way in the end, the good God gradually opens the eyes of his heart, so that he ends by understanding that it is God alone who gives him strength. Only then does man begin to give glory to God in the humility of a contrite heart. As David says: A sacrifice to God is a contrite heart (Ps. 50:19). Indeed it is from such difficulties in the struggle that humility, a contrite heart, meekness and gentleness are born . . . .[15].

This text is one of the most ancient in all monastic literature, and it is enough by itself to counter any idea that asceticism is some form of spiritual athletics, or that it is a matter of physical prowess. Nothing could be more contrary to true Christian asceticism. All Christian ascetic effort must bring about a sort of breaking of the heart; it must bring one to the point of nothingness of which we have spoken to make place for the power and the grace of Jesus. Only in the self-abasement and humility of the ascetic can this happen, for grace is entirely beyond our own efforts.

We do not speak, therefore, of ascetical prowess but of a true miracle of grace. This is the only correct term when we talk about the results of Christian asceticism—celibacy, fasting and obedience. When a man learns from his own experience that these are beyond him and that the self-denial involved in them is something he cannot do of himself, then God gives him the grace. The vocation of the ascetic, which is not necessarily that of every baptised person, is to give himself up to this miracle, to yield himself to it humbly in the joy of a broken heart, placing all his hope in the love of God.

We come back here to the original meaning of the word asceticism. We said that it means training, exercise, putting to the proof. But how does one exercise oneself in asceticism? What *is* this exercise about which we are talking? It is not a question of exercising one's own strength, in order to see how far one can go in asceticism. This matters little in Christian asceticism. It matters little to know whether or not you are capable of a particular ascetical practice. The ascetic must be borne along, not by his own strength but by God's grace. He must exercise himself in this grace and not in his own prowess or ability. He must know this grace truly and discern it correctly as it comes to him at each moment. If I am truly in touch with this grace, I can embark on the ascetical way without danger, for God calls me to it, and will not allow me to fail. But if I am out of touch with this grace, if I depend on myself, and am not borne up and carried by grace, if grace is not the motive force of my ascetic effort, then what right have I as it were to force God to intervene miraculously on my behalf? To do so would be both rash and foolhardy. To make grace my strength, to act only out of grace, is to be attentive at every moment to the interior impulse of the Spirit as he calls me in a particular direction.

As we proceed along the way of conformity with Jesus in the mystery of his death and resurrection, a certain measure of grace is given to us at every moment. This measure is very exact, and we cannot presume on it. Likewise we must take care not to go beyond it. But neither ought we allow ourselves to underestimate it. Often we do not come up to the measure which God gives so generously and so bountifully. As Isaiah tells us, when it comes to miracles, "The Lord's arm is not short" (59:2), and he is always ready to perform his wonders once again for his people.

But how can we correctly discern the measure of his grace? At the beginning of monastic life we are not able to do this, and that is why monastic tradition always attaches conditions to the practice of asceticism. The presence of a spiritual master is especially necessary. He is there to discern grace in us and to enable us to discern it in our turn. We can easily be deceived about the interior life. The mirage of pride can seem to be the inspiration of grace. To undertake the work of asceticism without being invited to do so by grace is to court failurre. More than that, it is to tempt God. St Benedict said that there is a way that seems right to a man, but in the end it plunges to the depths of hell. And in saying this he was quoting the word of God (cf RB 7:21; Prov. 14:12).

## 4. The monk's asceticism

### (a) Obedience

Obedience has already become part of a monk's life as he sets out to imitate Christ and to love him at the heart of the Church. But as well as this ecclesial aspect, obedience has another dimension —the ascetical—which will help him blaze a road to his own heart. We will consider it here under this aspect.

One of the Desert Fathers never tired of repeating this adage: "The will of man is a wall of brass between him and God"[16]. We can certainly say that our own will erects a similar wall between us and our deepest selves, between us and our heart, the centre of our being where God is, and which we so often overlook. One reason for this absence of our selves from ourselves is the multiplicity of our desires, which creates a sort of carapace, an impervious shell around the surface of our being. These desires entice us along many paths which do not always lead us to God. They distract us and prevent us from entering into ourselves in order to indentify peacefully with that deepest centre of our being where we already live in harmony with God, in his presence. It is this multiplicity of superficial desires which the ancient Fathers called "our own will". Whoever undertakes to renounce these desires goes about breaking down the wall of brass. He also disposes himself gradually to discern that desire which is his at a much deeper level of his being. This desire is at the root of his existence, and keeps him constantly united to God, who is sought in his person and in his will.

To unite oneself to this will, of which we are lovingly aware in our hearts, is already to pray in the simplest possible way. This is perhaps the most perfect prayer of all. Without this desire to conform absolutely to God's will, no true prayer is possible: "Thy will be done" (Mt. 6:10); "Not my will but thine be done" (Lk. 22:42).

(b) Celibacy

According to the teaching of St Paul, the primary aim of celibacy is to make us free for the Lord Jesus in love. The terms he uses to describe this freedom point very clearly towards prayer. In recommending celibacy, St Paul proposes that one "wait upon the Lord without distraction" (1 Cor. 7:35). Is there a better definition of uninterrupted prayer? Such prayer will one day be the most convincing proof of a celibacy which has reached its full flowering in the love of God.

Like all other forms of asceticism celibacy requires great care. The renunciation which it involves cannot but inflict a wound and that wound can continue to fester for a long time. There is much more to celibacy than simply resisting the desire for physical pleasure. The celibate creates an affective void within himself. This should not lessen or diminish his affective capacity. On the contrary, it should liberate it and put it at the service of the Lord Jesus and his Church, and especially at the service of the brothers with whom the monk lives. This will not be achieved in a single day. It is the end of a long slow haul, during which prayer predominates in the monk's life.

Whenever he meets temptation, the monk will spontaneously turn to prayer. He will feel the need of prayer in order to remain at peace, depending only on the power of God, for whose help he will pray without ceasing. Inevitably he will meet with difficult situations where he will find no way out but to cry to God, to call for help, to invoke doggedly the name of the Saviour. "Lord save us, we are sinking" (Mt. 8:25). How often will our prayer be little other than this? But this is enough. Gradually prayer will take on a more fundamental role. By the very fact of being continually in the Lord's presence, of clinging to him, of filling the silence by calling on his name, or of gazing steadfastly at his face, the faith which joins us to him will grow stronger and deeper. The solitude of celibacy will become a communion of love through prayer, and in this way a fulness will come into the heart of the monk which will be both human and divine. None of the personal richness that flows from love in the human being will be lost or lie fallow for the monk because of his celibacy. It will all be taken up and used to the full. By his deep bond of love with the Lord Jesus, he will be open to the fulness of divine life. This bond will differ from one person to another, according to the psychological make-up of each one. It will vary infinitely, just as human love does, for human love is only an imperfect reflection of the unfathomable riches of God's love.

To one person God will appear as friend or brother, to another master or father; to another an infinitely tender spouse. God *is* all of these at once, and is yet far more. In the face of his love all human comparisons fade. The saying of Jesus that anyone who has seen him has seen the Father can only be verified by experience (cf Jn 14:9).

(c) Community of goods

St Benedict is very strict about the individual poverty he requires of his monks. His choice of words is both vigorous and exhaustive. The monks are to possess nothing of their own, and the *Rule* sets out a precise list of objects which the monk of that period might legitimately have for his own use . . . book, writing tablet, stylus (RB 33). The abbot gives each monk what he needs. He takes care that no one lacks anything he needs. The monk on his part will never apply the possessive "my" to what is given him for his use, because everything must really be held in common. "All things should be held in the common possession of all" (RB 33:6). Anything with even the appearance of ownership is to be "completely uprooted" (RB 55:18). The abbot is told not to hesitate to inspect the cubicles of the monks. These were the only private places the monks of the sixth century had and the purpose of the inspection was to ensure that the prohibition of all private ownership was being respected.

How are we to explain this severity in the case of a man who otherwise shows himself so tolerant and considerate? The example of the primitive Christian community in Acts (Ac. 4:32) played an important part in St Benedict's thinking on the subject. He expressly mentions the punishment of Ananias and Saphira who tried to evade this sharing of goods (Ac. 5; RB 57).

But the main reason is that monastic tradition has always known that when the desire to possess is pursued determinedly, it will fill up that inner void which keeps a person open to the experience of God. And it is this latter that the monk proposes to himself before all. To have nothing of his own and to hold everything in common is the first and radical break in that wall of personal desires which separates us from God and from each other. On the other hand, to share everything with others is to be open to the good of the brethren. Being open to even one of his brothers shows that the monk is also capable of being open to God. At a deeper level still, having nothing of one's own is to be poor in the sense of needing others. But especially having nothing of one's own is to need God, who always leans down to those in distress. St Benedict wanted the monk to possess nothing so that he might expect everything from the father of the monastery (RB 33:5). Clearly he is here inviting the monk to confide his needs to the abbot. But behind the abbot is God, the Father and provider of all, who carries the poor in his heart. By having nothing of his own the monk becomes one of those who are dispensed from all care for the morrow, because God has promised to take care of them. This evangelical lack of care for the morrow often appears in ancient monastic texts. Practised in radical fashion within a

91

community it should make the monk wholly free for God and for prayer.

St Benedict does not seem to envisage a very marked material poverty for his communities as a whole. He is concerned instead to provide the monk with whatever is necessary so that the life of prayer can follow its course without hindrance. Yet he foresaw the possibility of a community being really poor. He considers that if God allows this, it is a grace and a special blessing. All monastic reforms have been concerned with poverty, as much at the level of the individual as of the community. This is often the best test of real evangelical fervour. Cîteaux was conspicuous for its poverty. The first Cistercians resolutely suppressed everything they considered superfluous in their way of life and even in the monastic liturgy of the time. The Cistercian life remains marked with this trait . . . a holy simplicity which unites the brethren to each other and to God.

(d) Silence

The Cistercians, particularly the Trappists, owe some of their fame to their legendary silence. The Trappist is known as the monk who never speaks. Although the details of the rule of silence have varied down the ages, a predilection for silence is always found among monks. Even today, speaking is subject to serious restrictions in a Cistercian monastery. There is, for example, the great silence of the night, which means that the time between Compline and Lauds is a special time for silence. During the rest of the day the monk speaks only to the extent necessary for work and for the good ordering of the house. Recreation is exceptional. Private conversation between monks is subject to previous permission or approval by the abbot. Conversations in small groups or with the whole community take place more frequently but in general not more often than once a week*.

The Cistercians owe this love of silence to St Benedict who gives more than mere principles on the matter in his *Rule*. He gives a general approach to the subject. He insists on the fact that the monk is above all a disciple and that means a man who listens. He

---

* This describes the practice in the author's monastery. Usage differs from one house to another.

should be silent so that he may be ever attentive to the word of God coming to him in Scripture and in the teaching of his abbot. Silence is also necessary if he is to be sensitive to the interior word which the Holy Spirit continually speaks in his heart. The asceticism of silence should create a space, an emptiness in the depths of his being, where God can be heard without any other noise. This is why silence should never be lacking to the monk. As St Benedict says: "Monks should diligently cultivate silence at all times" (RB 42:1). But in fact it is not always easy to find silence in a cenobitic community. Even when regulations were much stricter than they are today these could not be the ultimate norm. A law may help us discover our interior need for silence, but it cannot substitute for it. Silence is not completely real until it truly expresses the depths of our being.

Silence imposes itself on us inwardly in two ways. It issues from our poverty and it springs from our plenitude. Silence may sometimes be an expression of our poverty. This happens when we realise that we are not yet capable of speaking the word as we should. Jesus was very severe about the useless words a believer might speak thoughtlessly (Mt. 12:36). Speech is given to us to give testimony, to bear witness to the word of God or to give thanks and to bless God. But in fact speech has become one of the means whereby we most easily offend God and wrong our brethren. Hence some restriction of speech is a sign we have become aware of this, and that we sincerely want to speak only with mature deliberation and forethought. Such silence wells up from an emptiness within us, but it is an emptiness freely and fully accepted.

But there is another kind of silence which springs from a fulness within us. Isaac the Syrian writes:

> Let us force ourselves not to speak and in that way we will come to true silence. May God grant you to understand how silence is born. If you do this, I cannot tell you what light will shine for you . . . from the practice of silence is born that pleasure in repose and tranquillity which is true *hesychia*\*. And in such silence our tears

---

\* *Hesychia*: this word is a classic term in Greek spirituality and essentially it means contemplation, or meditation without images. The use of the *Jesus prayer* is perhaps the best known practice of *hesychia* in the Western Church.

come abundantly, at first in pain and then in joy. The heart already senses the sweetness and wonders of contemplation.;[17]

This silence is already prayer. Indeed, according to the same author, it is "the language of the ages to come"[18]. It witnesses to the fulness of the life of God within us, a fulness which must renounce all human words in order to express itself adequately.

For a while, maybe only the words of the Bible are used, or perhaps the name of Jesus, or—for one who has received the gift —only the incomprehensible babel of speaking in tongues. A moment comes when silence alone can express the extraordinary richness in our heart. Such a silence enfolds a person gently and powerfully and always comes from within. Prayer governs it and teaches us when we should be silent and when we should speak. It is very pure praise and at the same time it radiates outward to others. Such silence never hurts anyone. It establishes a zone of peace and quiet around the one who is silent, where God can be irresistibly felt as present. "Keep your heart in peace" says St Seraphin of Sarov "and a multitude around you will be saved"[19].

## (e) Watching

Following the example of Jesus, the monk is happy to give up part of his sleep in order to watch during the night. In the Cistercian tradition, based on the *Rule* of St Benedict, this watching takes place very early in the morning, before sunrise. After about seven hours sleep—enough for an adult in good health—the monk rises for Vigils which last in choir about an hour or slightly less. He will afterwards prolong this with a private vigil on the word of God, in *lectio* and prayer. By keeping watch every day, the monk tries to inscribe in the most basic rhythms of his body one of the fundamental attitudes of the monastic way—interior vigilance. Within his heart the monk is always on guard. He does not sleep. He watches. He is attentive to the thoughts and temptations which prowl about his heart inclining it to evil. He is attentive also to the least movement of grace which can signal God's approach. Is it not in the beautiful silence of the night that according to the gospel we will hear the cry announcing that the bridegroom is nigh? "Here is the bridegroom. Come out to meet him" (Mt. 25:6).

Every morning, even while it is still night, the monk rises joyfully to await the wonders that the Lord will work that day. But he does not keep watch only for himself. He watches indeed lest Jesus come to visit him during the day which is dawning, but he watches also on behalf of the Church and the whole world. As he waits for the dawn, he is on the alert for the slightest signs which could announce the imminent return of Jesus at the end of time. Jesus is always near and always on the point of returning. The monk proclaims this by his whole being as he persists morning after morning in his waiting. He proclaims too how urgent it is to draw the world from its sleep so that it may go out to meet him. It is then in the name of the whole world that the monk sets himself to wait in prayer. This opens him to God while at the same time enclosing him within himself.

At the crack of dawn, at the coming of the light, the monk stands on that frontier between the world which is passing away and the world which is coming. He looks towards the Saviour who always comes with mercy. Will he one day meet the Saviour in all truth to bear witness while still alive to the end of time? It does not matter as long as this meeting takes place every day in the obscurity of his faith and prayer. What is more, his prayer hastens the coming of Christ in glory. It draws the Church away from all those cares which distract it from its essential expectation of the great event. When the *last day* comes—that dawn which will never end—the prayer of the monk "Come Lord Jesus" (Rev. 22:30) will arise from the heart of the Church, endlessly repeated by the multitude of believers.

(f) Fasting

Fasting is one of the most ancient Christian practices, going back to Jesus himself. Monks have always held it in honour. St Benedict lays down in his *Rule* that the monks observe not only the fast of the Church, which in his time included the forty days of Lent, but also another fast of their own, only slightly less rigorous, from the feast of the Holy Cross in September to the beginning of Lent. He also enjoined a fast, if the work and climate allowed it, on Wednesdays and Fridays outside paschal time. This pattern has lasted with some variations down to our own day. Obviously, fasting

95

is not what it was when St Benedict wrote. In his day fasting meant that food was not taken until after midday or even after sundown. Today health and maybe also courage is weaker. So a fast is not considered broken by a little bread and drink in the morning and a frugal collation in the evening, with the main meal about midday. But here again the external ascetical practice has value only to the extent that it is an expression of and deepens the interior grace.

During his own fast of forty days, Jesus was confronted by the devil who came to attack him (cf Mt. 4:1-3). The monk in his turn undergoes a somewhat similar experience. He discovers that the desires he finds within himself can be summed up in his desire for food; that his appetite for food and drink can contain all other appetites. In trying to restrain himself in this area he touches on a principle of imbalance within himself which is beyond doubt a result of sin.

At the same time he finds that fasting restores integrity to a part of his being and frees a dynamism in him which had been shackled by other desires. All this happens to the extent that there is given him the power that comes from greater love, and that strength is given him by God. This process seems to be verified even on the natural plane in those religions and spiritual techniques which recognise the value of fasting. Here again, Jesus has invested fasting with a new meaning in proclaiming to the devil that if a man fasts he finds he does not live on bread alone but on every word that God utters (cf Mt. 4:4). Fasting leaves a person hungry and the aim of this hunger is to make him aware of and sharpen that spiritual hunger which gnaws at the heart of everyone; the hunger for the word of God. Anyone who fasts proclaims that earthly food cannot satisfy him as long as he does not receive this word in its fulness. Hunger for food has no other aim but to create a spiritual void by means of the body, wherein the word of God can be heard more clearly; and precisely because it is done through the body, it is the more effective, because it involves the whole person.

# Chapter 7

## LED BY THE SPIRIT

After these considerations on asceticism, which deepens our capacity for receiving the word of God, let us come back to *lectio* and prayer. We have seen how the word comes to us in *lectio* to awaken our heart. It makes us aware of that state of prayer within us which is first given us by the Holy Spirit. The power of the indwelling word creates in us a sensitivity to the life of God within. But that is not all, for it empowers us also to bring other gifts and other capacities into play.

### 1. *Ruminating on the word*

An ancient monastic custom decrees that when Scripture is proclaimed in the assembly, it is followed by a period of silence. It is good to see that this excellent practice has been restored by the Council in its reform of the liturgy for the faithful. After hearing the word, the monks recollect themselves and meditate on it. The same thing happens in the private reading of the word. As soon as the heart is touched by the word of Scripture, the reader pauses, wounded and struck by the sword of the word of God. The ancient writers used the Latin term *"compunctus"* to describe this. It means literally wounded or pierced as by a sword. The word pierces our heart and touches our very soul. This is what the letter to the Hebrews means when it speaks of the word of God being like a sharp sword (Heb. 4:12).

These are the most important moments in *lectio* and are already prayer. The monk pauses in his reading and as grace is given him this pause can be prolonged. He does not remain inactive nor is the word inactive in him. He simply gives himself up to it. If he repeats it quietly and slowly it will become clearer to the eyes of his heart. The Fathers created a picturesque vocabulary to describe this inner process. They speak of "ruminating" or "chewing on" the word, or they talk about "cradling it in one's heart". We can see what they are trying to say. By lovingly repeating the word I press it as one presses a fruit to extract all the juice from it. I nourish and feed myself with it, and in it I find strength. At the same time my heart is filled with new lights and I am seized by the word in a deeper way. The word impregnates my heart becoming connatural to me. My inner being is reborn by the power of the word which has pierced it, and which continually nourishes and strengthens it.

## 2. *The word becomes prayer*

This is already prayer in the sense that by ruminating on the word I find myself directly open to the power of God which works in me by it. But the word does more than that. It becomes prayer in me; and carries my word in turn to the Lord whom I worship. The Book of Psalms gives us a scriptural precedent for this prayer. The psalms occupy an altogether special place in the Bible. Like all the other books, the psalter contains the word of God. But the word of God in the psalms has changed its direction. It not only comes from God, it returns to him through the human heart. It is a word which God puts on man's lips so that by it he may unerringly invoke God. The psalmist had to have a heart impregnated by the word of God for this miracle to happen. God's word become prayer went out from him to return to God after recreating the psalmist's heart.

The psalms make up the greater part of the monastic office so that day and night they are ever on the monk's lips. St Benedict even insists that the entire psalter be said in a week, and he cites the example of the ancient monks who recited it every day (RB 18:23-5). The monk who sings the psalms today gives his heart and his voice to the fulness of the word, which springs up in prayer within him.

This is why vocal prayer, particularly the prayer of the psalter, demands less attention to the words than to one's own heart. Anyone whose heart is not awakened must give his attention to the words and try and make them his own so that they may touch him. But if his heart is already awakened he need only hear and listen to it. The words of the psalms speak to him of the movement of his own heart and enable him to recognise this. The meaning of the words is from within and they can be re-clothed with an ever more profound and luminous sense.

The words of the psalter refer not only to what God is doing in the individual human heart, but to what he does in the Church all during its long history and to the mystery of his will for the world. Through the words of the psalms, the heart of the monk expands to take in the whole history of salvation. He sings and gives thanks for the entire world.

## 3. *The prayer of a single word*

Anyone who prays the psalms this way with his heart and not with his head does not normally find it tiring. The multiplicity of words is not an obstacle to prayer. Yet the more he prays with his heart, the more the words of his prayer tend to simplify and become fewer. Eventually his prayer will be reduced to a very few words, a few verses of Scripture, or of the psalter, or perhaps even a single word. The fathers called this simplified prayer "the prayer of a single word".

This tendency, which is normal in all prayer, explains why a certain sobriety is characteristic of prayer in common. It is in personal prayer that the monk will truly "live with himself", as the ancients put it. It is there he will live in his own heart, and therefore it is essential that sufficient time for this personal prayer remains available to him. This prayer, flowing in silence and peace, will fill all his free time, making it truly leisure for God. The monk tries to keep himself quietly in the presence of the Lord. To this end he can use an actual image of Jesus, or be aware of his presence in his own heart. He repeats a brief word which gradually opens his heart to the extent that he gives himself to it. By this I mean that he will allow this word to fall within his heart; he will give it his whole attention, and he will not even consciously resist other thoughts or desires which may come to him, for this would itself become a distraction.

In whispering this single word a very dense interior silence gradually arises and in it God makes himself present. Then we will no longer pronounce the word as such, but will rather hear and listen in the depths of our heart to what is spoken by another. This is the voice of the Spirit of God praying in us with inarticulate groans. All we need do is abandon ourselves and give ourselves with the most interior faculties of our being to this presence of the Holy Spirit within us. When that happens we are truly children of God and led by the Spirit*. Our prayer will be none other than the prayer of the Spirit, the prayer of the Son to his Father. In this prayer we will find again the very source of our being, that secret entrance deep within us, which opens like a chasm to allow us to come to intimacy with God. As St Isaac the Syrian said: "We must penetrate into the interior of our heart if we are to find the door that opens on Paradise"[20].

The word which will support this prayer of a single word should be as simple as possible. It may be the name of God, or one of his attributes, a cry of confidence, of abandonment or of love. Many like to use only the name of Jesus, in which is embodied the very being of the Godhead (Col. 2:9), and which is the only name by which we find salvation (Ac. 4:12). The monk will want to live in that holy name, to rest in it for all eternity.

The prayer of a single word soon becomes a prayer without words. It will remain a very simple resting at the deepest part of our selves where God lets his presence be felt. The monk does not know how to describe this prayer. He is not able to talk of feeling, touching, hearing or indeed of contemplation. It is in fact all these together, but in a new and inexplicable way. God can if he will make the veil which separates us from him transparent, even here below. He can make it as transparent as possible, while still leaving it to be torn open at the moment of our death. This is a pure gift of his grace, a marvel of his mercy. No one can claim it or have a right to it, or do anything himself to force the hand of God. The Church and the Spirit confide the future to the monk. The long vigil of the monastic life, with its inevitable ups and downs, only disposes the monk for this enterprise which has been entrusted

* On this see Romans chapter 8.

to him as his own grace, for it is truly his own special work, the work of God. So the monk gives himself entirely to this waiting, of which he never grows weary, however pointless it may seem. He knows he is not deceived. Whatever his Lord sends, whether light or darkness, tender care or dereliction, the monk knows too that his waiting will never be entirely fulfilled in this world but only in the world to come—that world for which he ever yearns.

## 4. *The interior mansion*

To close this section about prayer, which is the essential activity of the monk, we would like to quote some passages from a treatise of an anonymous monk of the twelfth century. He says what we have been trying to say, but perhaps he says it more lucidly and more simply. The monk must as it were re-enter himself, he must find his own heart, he must learn how to know his heart in order to purify it and find the life of God there. Then he must settle himself there in love and contemplation, in a repose which nothing can disturb. There is no doubt that this treatise is one of the most beautiful examples of true hesychasm* in the literature of Western monasticism.

## TREATISE ON THE INTERIOR MANSION[21]

The following pages are a translation of a text by an anonymous twelfth-century Cistercian monk. Formerly attributed to St Bernard, it is now considered to be the work of another author. The style and language are of course markedly different to the rest of this book. It has been fairly freely translated from the original Latin, generally following the lines of the French of Dom André Louf. An attempt has been made to preserve the style and the rhythm of the original. Much of it is rather removed from the style of today's writing, but the essential message of the writer, the return to one's heart, is at the centre of the spirituality of this book and of the Cistercian school.

* See note on page 93.

## ENTER INTO YOURSELF AND FIND PEACE

Happy the soul which is rooted in the peace of Christ and grounded in God's love, and whose inner peace remains intact in the face of misfortune. No matter what storm should break upon it the silence of its inward calm is not disturbed, because, fired by an intimate and heartfelt sweetness, it is focused within by the sheer delight of its desire. At peace within itself and desiring nothing at all from outside, the soul abides totally within itself. Having gathered itself together, so to speak, so as to savour this intimate joy, it is reformed in God's image, which it venerates within itself and in which the divine mysteries are celebrated.

## DO NOT ALLOW YOURSELF TO BE TROUBLED

Your soul, having returned within itself, sees itself naked and desolate. It is seized with a horror and confusion beyond all telling. Conscious of the evil which it has done it cannot tolerate itself. It can find no rest in itself because it does not love him in whom it should root itself as in its proper soil, God, its only friend.

Gather together all the restlessness of your soul and all the distractions of your heart, and in God alone fix your whole desire. Let your heart be there where your treasure is to be found, that treasure so desirable and so worthy of being sought. This heavenly friend frequently enters into and dwells with delight in a peaceful heart and in the contemplative repose of a quiet mind: for he is Peace. Let each of you endeavour not to become divided within yourself. Recall God's mercies and you will be set alight by his love. Let your heart be upright, let it be pure and filled with sweetness. Let it weep for its own sorry state and for that of others. Let it be smitten with regret for the evil it has done and for the good it has failed to do. Let your spirit be free of worldly anxiety, of sensual pleasures and of thoughts of evil. Let nothing at all disturb its calm and repose: because Christ is Peace, and the lover of peace abides in peace.

But before everything else exercise yourself at length in self-knowledge. To no avail do you set the eye of your heart to see God if you are not accustomed to seeing yourself. It is necessary first of all to recognise those things which lie hidden in your own heart before you are fit to behold what lies hidden in the depths of God. If you would see God you must first of all clean your own mirror by cleansing your own soul. Having cleansed and examined carefully and at length your own mirror, some brightness of divine light will begin to shine in your soul, and an intense radiance of unusual vision will strike the eye of your heart. And the soul, set alight by this vision, will begin to contemplate both its own interior and the very depths of God. It will begin to love God and to cling to him, realising that he alone is happy who is loved by God. Without any doubt you will receive this singular gift if you flee the cares of the world and take care of yourself: that is to say, if you watch and seek to come to the knowledge of your real self.

Return, therefore, to your own heart and examine yourself with the greatest care, because from the knowledge of yourself you will be raised up to the contemplation of God. Perhaps you have already ascended, already returned to your heart, and there have learned to centre yourself. Should this not suffice, learn to dwell there, for this frequent exercise will transform it into something attractive for you.

Enter into yourself, then, and give yourself to dwelling as much as possible within yourself, assembling there the whole world of your thought and desires. When you have examined yourself attentively for a long time, and eventually discovered your real self, it will only remain for you to discern by divine light what you ought to be and what kind of house you should build in your soul for the Lord.

## BEYOND TROUBLE WE FIND JOY

Whoever gathers into one the dissipations of his soul, and channels all the movements of his heart into one desire for the eternal, has already entered into his own heart. He already dwells there with pleasure and discovers therein the most wonderful delights. Unable to contain himself for sheer joy he goes beyond himself, where through self-knowledge he comes to know God, whom alone he learns to love and in whom alone he desires to rest. When the love of Christ absorbs the whole affection of someone in this way, he forgets about himself, for his heart is afire with desire for Christ, and he frequently experiences spiritual intoxication. Present to God and stilled with admiration, he gazes on God's indescribable beauty; the power of the Father, the wisdom of the Son, the goodness of the Holy Spirit.

But soon he falls! Upon returning to himself he finds himself incapable of communicating anything of what he has seen to anyone. He remembers within his own heart the brightness of that heavenly light, the taste of that secret rapture, the inner repose and the mystery of that sovereign tranquillity. Sweetness and joy and all sorts of delights accompany this contemplation.

Let your conscience be good, upright, peaceful and pure, and God himself will want to become the guest of your heart. Attach yourself to him in faithful obedience lest such great majesty refuse to enter the innards of your heart. Such a conscience will find itself at rest . . . at peace with itself and pleasing to God.

## ALLOW YOUR CONSCIENCE TO LEAD YOU

Conscience is the knowledge of the heart; the knowledge of itself through itself, and the knowledge of other things which it discovers by knowing itself. Through its conscience the heart knows itself and many other things as well. This self-knowledge is called conscience, while that of other things is called knowledge.

You may live in a world of tears or laughter; of sorrow or of joy; you may even be nailed to the cross and face death. But if your conscience is good you will be undisturbed and will possess your soul in peace. Conscience is like a mirror in which the eye of reason can discern clearly what is good and what is not so good. You can come to a good conscience only by custody of the heart. For the heart of itself chooses either life or death. But if it should take a good look at itself, it will know what to do about itself. He possesses a noble kingdom indeed who is master of his own heart.

The heart is possessed of a natural movement and cannot remain immobile. For it to live is to move, and its movement is its life. But it sees that its movement is from God and so it realises that it does not move of itself. Rather of itself it is immobile.

Since it is God who moves you, allow yourself to be moved. Otherwise you will not be moved, but shaken. When you allow God to move you, you will contemplate the Trinity. O happy Vision, in which God will be in such a way that each of us will see him in one another!

## THE DISCIPLE

Conscience is for each of us a sort of book, for the correcting and enriching of which all other books exist. Happy the man who comes to the knowledge of himself. Many are the disciplines of man, but there is none better than that by which he knows himself. It is for this reason that I enter into my heart and remain there: so that I can examine my whole life and come to the knowledge of myself. I will pour out all my shame before the Lord that he may be moved to compassion. I will confess my sins to him in whose sight all things are open and laid bare, and to whom all things are present.

Listen, then, O most loving God, to my confession. When I go to pray I find my heart giving chase to incomprehensibly foolish thoughts. Day after day I try to remove from my heart the turmoil of these thoughts but cannot do so, for there is a great noise within me as they rush in to take over. I sin greviously whenever I forsake my heart, and I suffer greatly when it forsakes me—carried away as it is by a thousand thoughts and as many desires. These images soil my heart at night and wear it down. Nor does the heat of the flesh allow me any kind of rest. A pure heart create for me, O God; for even when I rest my heart is disturbed by the turmoil of temporal things. And even when my body is at rest my spirit rushes this way and that. Save me, Lord, from the enemy's hand. Wheresoever I turn, my wickedness follows me. And wherever I go, my conscience is there too, recording whatsoever I do. There is no escape whatever from its judgment, even though I know that this evil in my heart will be exposed eventually.

O Lord, be merciful to me because for my whole life I have drawn back in fear and trembling from those things which I discover within my heart: lack of devotion in church; permanent distraction of spirit and dissipation of life; eyes exhausted from looking this way and that as I take too much notice of everything that passes by. Woe is me for sinning in what should have been the occasion for correction. I have often promised to amend myself but have never kept my word, always returning to my sinful ways instead.

But I do not dare to fall into despair, O Lord, for you saved me on the cross. I thank you for coming to me, Lord, and showing me my sins. Thanks to your inspiration I have discovered the way back to my heart, and have come to the knowledge of myself. By your guidance I have returned to my heart, and having banished from it everything save God and my real self, have examined my whole life with great care and in great detail. And, to tell the truth, I have found it to be nothing other than a place of horror and a vast wilderness; that is to say, a conscience which has been long neglected, totally uncultivated, covered with brambles and thorns and filled with all kinds of rubbish. Meanwhile I am more frightened still that even in the monastery, in your presence, I find myself, O Lord, to be worse. Woe is me, for the Lord visits all my neighbours but never comes to me!

## THE SPIRITUAL FATHER'S RESPONSE

I rejoice for you because the Day Star from on high has come to visit you. You are not far from the kingdom of God, for the consciousness of sin is the beginning of salvation. Trust in the Lord, since the humility of a clean and full confession will supply for any lack of fervour and goodness of life in you. The Holy Spirit frequently visits the heart which has been smitten by the tears of penitence. He establishes therein a certain familiarity with God so that it experiences his visits more often, and by them not only is it consoled but it is filled with a joy beyond all telling. If, however, you turn a blind eye to your own sorry state you remove yourself from God's mercy. Far from entertaining an evil thought in your heart, reject it immediately; for the evil will bring to birth a sense of delight, delight will give birth to consent, consent to action, action to habit, habit to necessity and necessity to death.

The conscience of man is a bottomless abyss. For just as an abyss cannot be emptied out, neither can the heart of man be emptied of his thoughts; they oscillate continually within it. The heart of man is a sea vast and wide, with its moving swarms past counting (cf Ps. 103:25). As the reptile creeps about surreptitiously and slithers along in intricate windings, in the same way do poisonous thoughts infiltrate and spread through a man's conscience so that he knows not from where they have come nor where they are going. He who never examines himself will never know himself, nor will he ever pray.

Prayer is devotion of the heart, the turning to God through pious and humble affection. Humble from the intimate knowledge of its own weakness; pious from the acknowledgement of God's mercy. And so when you would pray, enter alone into the solitude of your heart, and with your spirit and mind recollected and emptied of cares, go into the place of prayer. Stand in the presence of God and penetrate the heavens by the directness of your prayer. Acknowledge your needs, and implore God's loving kindness. You must pray without ceasing. Happy the soul which gathers together all the distractions of the spirit. When you pray call on the Holy Spirit to help you. Prayer is of the heart rather than of the lips. God listens to the heart of him who prays rather than to the words uttered by the lips.

## THE DISCIPLE

Therefore, O my soul, restrain the turbulence of your heart and focus the multitude of your thoughts and affections on desiring only the one true joy.

I will enter alone the solitude of my heart and converse a little with it. I will ask it about itself and about those things which concern it. My heart is perverse, vain and changeable; is cunning to the finest degree. It is for ever on the move, always seeking rest where there is none. I have sought rest in every possible thing but found it nowhere. Having eventually returned to myself I find no rest there either, because my spirit is exceedingly fickle, unstable and wandering, like a leaf blown about by the wind. Having examined myself closely I find that I cannot tolerate myself. Moreover, there are even more terrible things hidden away in the depths of my heart which I am still too afraid to acknowledge.

## THE SPIRITUAL FATHER

No discipline is better than that by which a man comes to the knowledge of himself. Leave aside all other things and take a look at yourself, take a trip through your own heart and linger there awhile, so that from the knowledge you gain of yourself you may come to the knowledge of God. He who does not know himself cannot judge anything accurately. O guardian of the heart, if you are not yet fit to enter into yourself, how can you properly assess those things which are above and below you? Come back to yourself before attempting to judge that which is above you. You must first of all return to yourself, enter into your own heart and come to know your soul. Then, as the result of a realistic self-knowledge, you will come to the knowledge of all that is in heaven, on the earth and under the earth.

## THE DISCIPLE

My God seeks and loves solitude. Let me therefore flee the comforts and ways of men so that God might come to dwell in the inmost part of my heart. Let me accustom myself to think of and to love only interior things, so that I may hear what the Lord my God is saying within me. Behold I am here, O most loving Lord. I am with you, within my own heart. I have been preoccupied for so long in external things that I have been unable to hear your voice within me. But having returned to myself now, I have approached you so as to be able to listen to you and to speak with you. Speak, then, most merciful Lord, your servant is listening.

O my soul, if you would be loved by God, refashion his image within you and he will love you. Restore his likeness within you and he will desire you. Acknowledge in yourself the venerable image of the holy Trinity. You can bring it to birth in your own heart and also in the heart of another. You can conceive it from your own heart and from the mouth of another. When you beget you are a father; when you conceive you are a mother.

Happy the man who can have God as son whenever he wishes. The holy soul, true friend of the beloved, will always sigh with the greatest longing for the coming of the beloved. Such a one will always be open and ready to receive him without any delay whatever, when he knocks. It is one thing to enter with him, but quite another to go out to meet him. In the former case, the soul returns to itself, and accompanied by its beloved, penetrates to the inmost core of its own heart. In the latter case it is led beyond itself and is raised up to the contemplation of sublime things. To return to itself is to collect and centre its whole self within itself. To go out is to pour its whole self outside itself. To examine yourself is to allow your heart to be inflamed by ardent sentiments so that the beloved is brought to the inmost core of the heart, where he is given pride of place because he is loved above all things from the very depths of your being.

Apply yourself to this, and hasten to bring him to the most intimate and secret depths of your heart. This inmost retreat of the heart has such hiding places that no evil pleasures could oust the sentiments of pure love therefrom. Seek to make him penetrate to the innermost parts of your heart and of your very self; for then you will be able to pursue him to the heights. Gather yourself to yourself, and repose only in the desire to enjoy his divinity.

Desire impetuously to contemplate him face to face. What burning desires, what deep yearnings, what joys inflame the soul which has been given to penetrate the divine light to the very glory itself which illumines the angelic heights, so that it becomes transformed from clarity to clarity into a like image!

If you would give yourself to this delightful exercise, learn to rest in your body and in your heart—there in its most profound care, in the sabbath of sabbaths.

# Chapter 8

## "LABORIOUS LEISURE"

The ancients had a phrase to describe life in the monastery which it is almost impossible to translate into English—"*otium negotiotissimum*". Perhaps the best way to put it into our idiom would be to say that the monk must always be at rest before the Lord yet never be idle. For to rest before the Lord is itself work, and the monk's work does not separate him from God or prevent him from hearing the word of the Lord, and so he is never idle.

The most intimate and most important part of monastic life is continual prayer. This indeed is its very heart. We must now see how this prayer is woven into the texture of every day, and how it gains from the balanced rhythm of the life. The monk's day is traditionally composed of three elements: the office, *lectio* and manual work. These three alternate with each other in a rhythm that is basically the same in every monastery, and which corresponds to that established by St Benedict for his own time. We have already set out the principal points of the monk's daily round and need not cover it again in detail. It will be enough if we recall certain constants of the timetable, whose importance lies in the original and creative way they resolve the tension between the various activities of the monk. On the one hand he must pursue interiority and prayer; on the other hand he must work for his living and be busy about material things. Without these latter he cannot live. The problem is to establish a balance between prayer and work. The old monastic adage is "pray and work" and this sums up the monk's life. This balance is important for the life of the individual monk and for the community as a whole. It guarantees the authenticity of the life led by both.

## 1. *The prayer of the hours*

The first element of this balance is assured by the way in which monastic tradition has arranged the prayer of the hours as a crown around the day. The tradition here takes up a practice that goes back to the very first Christian communities. It appears that they periodically interrupted the day's work with a brief pause for the word of God and for prayer. These interruptions were so arranged as not to be too far apart, and thus work and prayer were interspersed throughout the day.

The monk's day begins very early when the night is not yet over. For the Cistercian today this varies from one country to another, but generally he rises between three and four o'clock in the morning, sometimes a little earlier. As soon as he is up the monk heads for the church where the community prayer of the night, called Vigils (formerly Matins) is about to begin. This consists of psalms and readings, as we have already said, and lasts from about three-quarters of an hour to an hour. It is preceded or followed by personal prayer in common, which lasts for anything from a quarter to three-quarters of an hour. Some communities intersperse this personal prayer in the elements of the office itself. This is the beginning, which sets the monk on his way for the day. Until work starts usually about eight or nine o'clock, the prayer of the office, private prayer and reading, succeed each other. The office of Vigils is followed by a long interval of an hour and a half to two hours, entirely given up to private reading and prayer. Towards the end of this interval the office of Lauds, the solemn praise of the morning, is celebrated. Frequently this will be followed by mass concelebrated with the whole community. The mass is the culminating point of the whole day, and the best hour of the day, the first of the morning, is given to it.

Then work begins, but not without the word of God. The ancient hermits of Egypt who wove their baskets in the desert, frequently interrupted their work to recite a few psalms or a few verses of the New Testament which they knew by heart, following these with a moment's recollection. They then set to work again. During the work they often prayed with their lips and if this were not

possible at least with their hearts. Monks had the habit of season-
ing all work with the word of God, peferably a few verses of
Scripture. This was the practice of the hermits. Of necessity work
was more extended for the cenobites. But following a custom which
went back to the synagogue and perhaps to the Lord himself, they
interrupted their work every three hours or so for prayer. They
assembled in the oratory for a short pause to hear the word of God
and to recite a few psalms. St Benedict retained this custom and
consecrated it in the prayer of the "little hours". The psalms of
these little hours were always the same, so that the monks knew
them by heart, and did not have to carry heavy manuscripts with
them to work. If necessary the little hours were celebrated outside
the oratory, at the place of work, and even in the fields. Similarly
if the monks were on a journey, they would stop at the time of prayer
so as not to allow it pass without turning to God.

St Benedict set down four little hours in the day; about six o'clock
in the morning, about nine o'clock, about midday, and about three
in the afternoon. Then he prescribed a fifth hour just before the
community retired in the evening. Apart from the first of these,
all are still recited in Cistercian monasteries. Some communities
group the three daylight hours into one and recite it at noon. There
is no doubt that this regular interruption of work, be it manual
or intellectual, is a constraint. But it is also a source of great blessing
in the monk's life. St Benedict was emphatic that at the first signal
of the bell calling to office, each should depart immediately from
the place of work, leaving undone whatever he was doing. Nothing
is to be preferred to the work of God, that is to the office (RB 43:3).
This pithy formula expresses something that should come from
the heart of every monk. It echoes another saying of St Benedict:
that "the love of Christ should come before all else" (RB 4:21).

To love Christ is to love prayer, to be ready at every moment
to drop everything and hurry to that place where God is about to
speak his word to us and is waiting for our response. The prayer
of the hours woven around the monastic day, allows the monk to
reaffirm his loving choice very concretely several times a day.
Whatever the exigencies of work, nothing is more important than
the one work for which the monk has come to the monastery—

the work of God. This is so called not only because it is entirely devoted to God, but also and especially because God is himself at work in the heart which is open to him.

## 2. "... let them have specified periods for manual labour" (RB 48)

When St Benedict composed the timetable for his monks he gave manual labour a very important place in it, reserving six to eight hours a day for it. In the same way, when the first monks of Cîteaux left Molesmes to found the new monastery manual work was one of the important pc ts on their programme of reform. Today the Cistercian monk sets aside five to six hours a day for work, which in most cases is hard manual labour.

History remembers the monks of the West as hard-working and inventive men who deserve well of society for their achievements in agriculture, learning and the arts. Yet it is a curious fact that manual work was not always accepted by monks as being part of their way of life.

Before St Benedict there were monks who claimed thàt they should abstain from work entirely on the grounds that such work was contrary to the better part enjoined by the Lord, which was of course prayer. They also claimed that work was opposed to the evangelical precept of taking no care for the morrow, after the example of the birds of the air who neither sow nor reap (Mt. 6:26). The reasoning behind this was specious but the philosophy of idleness is always attractive to some. The personal example and vigorous teaching of several spiritual masters was needed before manual work was accepted generally in monasteries.

Even then some restrictions were necessary if work was not to interfere with the heart of monastic life, which is an exclusive application to God in prayer. Thus St Basil and John Cassian still forbade field work as contrary to interior recollection. St Benedict however did not agree with this. He accepted the possibility that the monks might have to save the harvest. This is more than mere toleration of an unfortunate situation, in that he consoles his monks who are obliged to go out to work in the fields, by setting before them the example of the Apostles and the Fathers, who worked with their hands so as not to be a burden on anyone. He goes on to say that "they are really monks if they have to work with their hands" (RB 48:7,8).

## 3. *"In all things — rest"*

The debate began again in the twelfth century when the Cistercians" fervour for manual labour led to the reproach that they had exchanged the contemplative leisure of Mary for the active work of Martha. The objection was predictable. It suggested that the Cistercians had sacrificed the essence of the monastic life, prayer of the heart, in favour of an element which was merely secondary. The white monks reacted vigorously by trying to explain how manual work was no obstacle to the repose which the monk ought to seek in the cloister. They held that if properly understood and carried out in a right spirit work could foster this interior repose.

On this subject, Guerric the abbot of Igny has a brilliant synthesis in his sermon on the Assumption which calls for quotation. He has chosen for the sermon a provocative title — "In all things — rest". The liturgy of the day applied this text of the Book of Wisdom to the Virgin Mary, prompted no doubt by the gospel of "the better part" traditionally read on that day. Guerric uses these texts to explain how manual work and the repose of contemplation can go together in a Cistercian monastery. He quotes St Augustine to the effect that if we are to achieve this repose, whose fulness is reserved for the life to come, we must resign ourselves here to endure the work of Martha. He says:

> Happy is he who in all his labours and in all his ways seeks blessed rest, always hastening, as the Apostle exhorts, to enter into that rest. For desire of it he afflicts his body, but already prepares and disposes his spirit for that rest, being at peace with all men as far as it lies with him. Giving the preference, where his will is concerned, to the rest and the leisure of Mary, to the extent that necessity demands he accepts the toil and the business of Martha, yet does this with as much peace and quiet of spirit as he can, and always brings himself back from that manifold distraction to the one thing necessary.

> A man of this sort is at rest even when he is working, just as on the contrary the godless man has to work even when he is resting.

Guerric can conclude, speaking from his own experience "in all things, therefore, I have sought rest, even in work"[22].

The debate slowly died down. The Cistercians were convinced that it was possible and even desirable to join work and repose, saying that where Martha was united to Mary, there the saying of the wise man is fulfilled—that he who works must always rest and he who rests must also work. It was Peter of Celle, not a Cistercian, who said: "He who rests must also work"[23]. We could take this to mean that the one who gives himself to prayer is invited to join all those who are at work. But this is not exactly what he meant. The author rather wishes to say that rest in God is itself extremely active, and that the leisure of monastic life should be entirely occupied with the inner activity of the heart, which is prayer. He who is engaged in exterior work should direct his work towards interior repose, but he who gives himself up to this repose should not forget that it is difficult and demands application. And *that* is the "very laborious leisure" which we have been talking about in this section.

## 4. *Work is healing*

In practice monastic work posed no problem except in the Mediterranean and in the East. The Celts, the Anglo-Saxons and the Germans, whose more active genius accommodated the demands of work more easily, do not seem to have had any difficulty in integrating work into a truly spiritual experience. They instinctively sensed that work was beneficial and a desirable counterpart of all spiritual effort, a guarantee of normality when used in a sane and balanced fashion. We have heard of a psychiatrist who when dealing with a loquacious patient allows him talk about his symptoms and problems for a while, and then interrupts him brusquely with the question: "What material do you work with?". Invariably the patient is nonplussed, and does not know what to say. Indeed most patients do not understand the question. The doctor then goes on to explain that if we are to keep in touch with reality, we must work with

114

some material substance that resists us, and against which we have to pit ourselves to reshape it.

Monastic life puts the same question to every aspirant who in his generosity can easily be led into a false spirituality far removed from the realities of everyday life, and by the same token far from God, the supreme reality. So the question "What material do you work with?" can be asked of every spiritual person. Whatever it is—the soil, clay, wood, water, metal, cheese or chocolate, the monk needs this simple material to measure himself against, every day. He will thus be kept in contact with reality, for these things come from the hand of God and are solidly rooted in the earth from which they are drawn, and of which they remain part. ∂

Work is more than just an element of psychological balance. In the Christian perspective it has redemptive value. The Book of Genesis tells us how God cursed the earth after the sin of our first parents, and how work was imposed on them so that the earth might bring forth the fruits which man needed in order to live. Thereafter all work shares in that suffering which has invaded the world after sin. At the same time work redeems the sin and helps build a new world. All work with its effort and constraint is marked with a double sign. The monk is not dispensed from either of these aspects of work. He is happy to share in the lot of all men, and in this way to bring his own small contribution to the work of redemption, in solidarity with all.

This holds true especially for hard and humble work which really *is* manual labour and comes from real poverty. Monastic communities are facing the same economic problems as the rest of the world. They must work if they are to live. The economic circumstances of the monastery may not be always those the monks might have chosen. Real work by which we truly earn our bread is a feature of poverty. St Benedict explicitly ruled out begging as a form of support for his monks, because he wished them to imitate the Apostles and the ancient Fathers who supported themselves by the work of their hands.

While work has its burdensome aspect it should also provide an occasion for prayer. Hardship shared with others for the sins of the world becomes a true sacrifice of praise. It brings its own contribution to that uninterrupted prayer out of which the monk's day is woven. Blessed Guerric remarked that work is useful to calm the heart and pacify it: "Work is a load by which, as ships are given weight so hearts are given quiet and gravity, and in it the outward man finds a firm foundation and a settled condition."[24] John Cassian spoke of work as an anchor which can stabilise the boat of our heart on the tumultuous waves of our thoughts[25].

In absorbing some part of the monk's energies and in channelling them towards a service which is useful to the brethren, manual work frees the inner man for that work which is properly his own. It ensures that he does not just spin like a top, frittering his time away. Nothing is more quieting for the spirit than hard manual work, which brings us into contact with matter, preferably in the open air and far from noise. The monk comes away from it with his body tired but his heart refreshed and eager for the inner work of the word and prayer. Did not St Bernard confess that he learned more from the boulders and the beeches than from books?[26]
;William of St Thierry, his friend and biographer, said of him that "outwardly he was entirely given up to work, but inwardly he was entirely given up to God"[27]. Some monks can live very simply united to God in a life style where work and fraternal service predominate. But this is the fruit of a maturity which should not be taken for granted or easily assumed.

## 5. *The search for balance*

The controversies which have surrounded manual work in the monastic life show clearly that it poses a delicate problem for each monastery and for each monk. Work is not only necessary for our livelihood, but it is a valuable help to the life of prayer. At the same time it brings with it the risk of taking over a community or a monk and leading to an overtaxed life. In the monastic life the balance between repose and work is something that only grace can achieve. By the same token this balance can be a good criterion of whether or not a monk's life is happy and fulfilled. If this balance is to be achieved, a taste for *lectio* and prayer must take first place with the monk. They must be his preferred activities, so that when he is not working he naturally turns to prayer and *lectio*. It is as though he had such a bent for these that he turns to them despite himself. It is important of course that the monk's work be real work which genuinely engages his talents and creative activity. At the same time, the monk must remain detached from work to avoid reaching a point where he would consider work the better part. This better part is always reserved for the work of God, to which nothing, absolutely nothing, is to be preferred (RB 43:3).

The solution to all this will not be found on our first day in the monastery. For those who serve the community in positions of responsibility, the balance will be found only through faith and abandonment to the Lord, who is at work in their material occupations in a way that far surpasses anything they could hope for.

In all this the monk must rely on two certainties which come from the word of God. Firstly, as long as duty does not clearly indicate otherwise, he should always prefer repose in prayer. Secondly he should always seek the Kingdom first, believing that all else will follow. A word about each of these.

Mary was praised by Jesus because she chose this repose at his feet—the better part. The Lord waits for this same response and this same choice from the monk regardless of his circumstances or the difficulties of his situation. This holds even though he may be led by his natural desire for activity to chose the less good part. Jesus tells us in the gospel to set our minds on God's Kingdom and his justice before everything else (Mt. 6:33). It is then that everything else will be given us. The Lord is always ready to give this increase to anyone who tends ceaselessly towards the kingdom, who puts his whole heart into seeking the grace essential to the kingdom. He will renew this miracle today for the monk and for the community who put their hope in him.

In the final analysis we must admit that the balance between work and prayer in the life of a monastery has something miraculous about it. God does not cease to renew this miracle for those who put their trust in him and who reserve all their leisure for him. If the monk uses his "*otium negotiotissimum*", his leisure which is full of the work of God, for God alone, then God will free his heart for this miracle.

117

# Chapter 9

## THE BATTLE LINE OF BROTHERS

As we have already said, the Cistercian does not walk alone on the way he is trying to follow. He enters a community and commits himself to it. He joins an abbot and brethren who will, as St Benedict says, be brought together with him to eternal life (RB 72:12). From the early days in the desert, monks have grouped themselves into communities. St Pachomius is famous as the initiator of this kind of life. After he had spent a long time in solitude with only a few disciples, an angel appeared to him suggesting that he set up a community so that a greater number of brethren could be saved.

Whether this vision actually took place or not, the story shows us that Pachomius believed that he had a mission from God to establish this new way of life. He is thus the father of what came to be called "the holy *koinonia*". This word, taken from the Greek New Testament, means communion, and suggests the spiritual attitude of the brethren who live together. The *koinonia* or communion that exists between the brothers is an image of that other communion which exists between the persons of the holy Trinity (cf 1 Jn 1:13). After Pachomius the cenobitic way of life became accepted and innumerable monks found the fulfilment of their vocation in it. St Benedict gives evidence of great respect for the solitary life in his Rule, and he leaves the door to it open. However, he writes only for cenobites, monks who live in community, and he calls these "the strong kind" (RB 1:13). They engage in the spiritual combat together, in what he calls "a battle line of brothers", in which each monk can count on the support of his companions (RB 1:5). When Cîteaux expanded in the twelfth century, another expression gained currency, and it shows even more clearly what cenobites attribute to and expect from the common life. The monastery then came to be called a "church". So the monastery of Cîteaux became the "church that is at Cîteaux". In this way the monastic community expressed its conviction that it was a sign of the people of God. It saw itself once again as a people whom God had called from the world to be re-created anew in the desert. It affirmed at the same time the special bonds which attached it to the great Church of Jesus Christ, which continued the battle in the midst of the world. The Church of the desert and the Church of the world together make up the one people of God, and each in its own fashion keeps up the assault on the Prince of Darkness, about which the Book of Revelation tells us (cf Rev 12).

## 1. *A lover of the brethren and the place*

The phrase is first found in the primitive Cistercian documents as a panegyric on one of the first abbots of Cîteaux—he loved the brethren and the place. The same thing strikes anyone who today comes into contact with a monastic community for the first time. The love which the monks have for each other and for the place in which they live is palpable. A Cistercian community is brought into being by this double bond. The tie between the brethren and the tie to the monastery are made the object of a vow by St Benedict, which he calls stability. The vow of stability is in fact one of the elements of the Rule which are original to it. Benedictines and Cistercians take this vow of stability today and it binds them for better or for worse to their community for life.

There can be no doubt that St Benedict had no time for so-called pilgrim monks who in his time wandered about from one monastery to another. He calls them *"gyrovagues"* or wanderers, and described their behaviour as capricious and unstable. He wanted to preserve his monks from this itch to wander about from one monastery to another, from one province to another, under all sorts of pious and fallacious pretexts (cf RB1 and 66). St Benedict had little time for monks who are always on the road. He knew by experience that the monastic enterprise is not brought to a successful conclusion by such conduct. He remarks laconically: "(There should be) no need for the monks to roam outside, as this is not at all good for their souls" (RB 66:7). In view of this he ordered that the monastery be so built that everything the monks need is within the enclosure (RB 66:6). The monastery is to be a place of stability and peace, a workshop wherein each monk should be assiduously devoted to his task, the work of God. The lawgiver sums up the interior attitude of the monk in a brief but profound formula when he says that the monk is to work in the enclosure of the monastery and stability in the community (cf RB 4:78). Both these elements are essential to the monastic way of life.

So the person who enters a Cistercian monastery joins a community which has roots in the place. The seniors have lived there for maybe half a century, and they have become part of a much longer tradition. The Cistercian heritage is transmitted by a particular way of life, by a particular spirit, even though the community itself cannot be reduced to this, just as it cannot be identified with the sum of all its members. It treasures its own past and tradition, which it recalls and safeguards with love, for they are its support. A community passes on its heritage from one generation to another with every day of its life, and in this way its spirit lives forever.

If someone decides to join a group of monks already searching for God he decides in fact to put himself in their school. As we have seen, his apprenticeship is done in the novitiate. But right from the beginning and even more so later on, the whole community is actively involved in forming him. The monks, especially the seniors who have lived the ordinary daily life of the monastery for years, have their experience to pass on to others who come after them. They in turn have drawn from those who were in the community before them. Thus the whole community shapes the spiritual life of its members.

## 2. *The abbot and the seniors*

The abbot occupies a special place in the community. Before his election he was simply one of the brethren, but his fellow monks have chosen him as abbot because they believe he has those charisms of discernment and prudence needed to guide the community. A neighbouring abbot comes to instal the newly elected abbot in his seat in the chapter room where he dispenses the word. As soon as this is done all the monks come up to him to renew their promise of obedience. From that moment, in the words of St Benedict, they consider the abbot as holding the place of Christ in the monastery (RB 2:2).

Christ has given his life for love of the flock and the abbot's duty is above all one of love. He will seek to be loved rather than feared (RB 64:15). He will always come down on the side of mercy rather than justice (RB 64:10). He will be the living bond of love between all the brothers. Twice a day, at Lauds and at Vespers, he will recite the Our Father aloud with the community so that everyone may hear those awesome words "forgive us as we forgive others" (RB 13:12) and so be led to make peace with each other before the sun goes down (RB 4:73). It is thus that the abbot, like Christ, will come to be loved by all the brethren with "an unfeigned and humble love" (RB 72:11).

He will proclaim the word of God tirelessly. St Benedict calls him a teacher (RB 5:6). In public and in private he is to teach the ways of the Lord and of spiritual experience. His words are put into the hearts of the disciples like a leaven of holiness (RB 2:5). Slowly and gradually hearts will grow by the grace the word of the abbot brings them. In the mind of St Benedict, the abbot also has a duty to correct, and even sometimes to punish (RB 2:29). The *Rule* recalls that the father who ignores or goes along with the faults of his sons does not truly love them (RB 2:29). But this must always be done with kindness and moderation, and, as St Benedict says, "in charity" as proof of genuine love (cf RB 64:14).

If the abbot is to be a spiritual father to the monks—and especially if the practice of individual spiritual direction is common in the community—he needs others to help him. In most cases this is so simply because of the size of the community. Freedom of conscience must also be respected. So for help of a more personal kind the brethren can address themselves to either the abbot or to one of the "seniors", spiritual men in the community able to give the same service. To assist the abbot in his government, St Benedict suggested dividing up the community into groups of ten, each group having at its head a dean appointed by the abbot (RB21)*.

To a young abbot who complained of the burden of his task, St Bernard replied:

> This is the burden of souls which are sick, for those which are well do not need to be carried and so are no burden. You must understand that you are especially abbot of the sad, faint-hearted, and discontented among your flock. It is by consoling, encouraging, and admonishing that you do your duty and carry your burden and, by carrying your burden, heal those you carry. If there is anyone so spiritually healthy that he rather helps you than is helped by you, you are not so much his father as his equal, not so much his abbot as his fellow. Why then do you complain that you find the company of some of those who are with you more of a burden than a comfort? You were given to them as abbot not to be comforted but to comfort, because you were the strongest of them all and, by God's grace, able to comfort them all without needing to be comforted by any.[28]

## 3. Community life and solitude

One characteristic of Cistercian monasticism is the balance between community life and solitude. Cîteaux and La Trappe have given these elements a special emphasis so that one complements the other. For the monk today solitude consists in a life style that is withdrawn from the world as was that of the first Cistercians in the marshes and forests around Cîteaux. Today the monk still leaves the cloister only by way of exception, and receives visits only from his relatives. News comes into the monastery only to a limited extent, mainly to give the monks an opportunity of praying for the great issues of the world today.

The common life is no less demanding. The first Cistercians seem to have wanted to revive the experience of the primitive Christian communities in which all things were held in common. The invitation to do this was met radically in the daily life of the new monastery at Cîteaux. The brethren prayed together, worked

---

* Monastic history shows little evidence that this was ever done on any considerable scale; but it is being looked at more favourably today in large monasteries.

together in the monastery, read and meditated on the word in a common room or in the cloister, took their meals in a common refectory and slept in a common dormitory. This latter held until our own time when the sole privacy of the monk was a small cubicle in which he slept in the large dormitory. Only recently have some monasteries introduced private rooms. This has favoured calm and quiet for reading and meditation, but it would be wrong to credit the Cistercians with a spirituality of the cell which is foreign to their essential charism. In a life where everything is done in common, silence is essential if solitude is to be maintained. We have already seen that silence is a distinctive mark of the Cistercian monastery. It still strikes visitors today as it did in the twelfth century. At that time, William of St Thierry recorded how when he first came to Clairvaux he was struck by this astonishing picture of intense community life lived in silence.

> From the moment when having come down the mountainside, I arrived at the Abbey of Clairvaux, I could sense the presence of God. By the simplicity and humility of the buildings the silent valley spoke of the simplicity and humility of those who lived there—the poor of Christ. Then as I went further into this valley full of people, of whom none was idle but all engaged in their various tasks, I realised that the silence here is as complete by day as it is by night, and apart from the noise of the work or the sweet sound of the praises of God, there is nothing to be heard. The effect of such silence in the midst of such activity on those who come here, is so profound that not only do they forbear from speaking idle and vain words, but they even maintain a reverent silence themselves. Even though the number of monks was great, each one was alone. A well-ordered charity brought it about that though the valley was filled with men, each one was alone and solitary. Just as a man whose spirit is disordered is never alone, even when by himself, but is ever in the midst of a turbulent crowd; so those who are united in the spirit and submit to the rule of silence, are always solitary and alone in their own hearts, even though they are surrounded by a crowd.[29]

While community life and solitude are closely linked in the daily life of the Cistercian, the interpretation and the emphasis given to each can legitimately vary. Is the Cistercian a solitary who lives in community or a cenobite whose cell is altogether interior in the silence of his heart? Both these vocations certainly exist together in the same community. For example, there are some quasi-eremetical vocations which find their fulfilment, their development and their flowering in an intensely common life where strict silence guarantees solitude. St Bernard had already remarked in his time that spiritual hermits are to be found in any Cistercian community.

> In every monastery we can find the four kinds of monks who are mentioned by St Benedict. We find the cenobites who consecrate themselves entirely to obedience to the seniors, in the practice of the common rule of the monastery and the common life. Then there are anchorites who in the words of Job, build themselves solitudes, in this sense that while they live entierly with their brethren, they also give themselves up entirely to interior contemplation.[30]

While this is true it does seem that the Cistercian way is normally offered to those who are true cenobites, but whose principal attraction is to silent and contemplative prayer. Such men desire the presence of their brothers, and live intensely the spiritual communion that is community life. They share all the realities of the common life with those around them. But their communion with their brothers has no need of a torrent of words. On the contrary, it is in recollection that each assumes responsibility for the common life. Each one knows that at certain times the most eloquent sign of fraternal love and the best gift he can offer his brothers is silence.

## 4. The apprenticeship of love

We have already seen that Cîteaux aimed to become a school of love — a school of charity. Life in community is one of the most important elements in such a concept. Thanks to the common life, this school does not remain in the realm of ideas and theory alone. It is a school of real life which provides an apprenticeship to love. One learns how to love by loving. Love must of necessity pass through trial and thus be more effectively matured. St Benedict speaks of false brethren and there is no doubt that the monk will sometimes feel that he has met these in community, perhaps during a time of crisis. He will have to learn to endure their insults patiently (RB 7:43).

Sometimes indeed things appear distorted because we can get everything out of proportion if we are troubled. Nowhere does there exist a community in which trials and tensions do not threaten to break the bonds between brothers. The monk knows this and he realises that it is by means of these trials that the depth of the evangelical commitment of the community will be tried and perfected.

St Bernard says: "it serves little to live together if we remain separated in spirit. It serves little to be united in one place if we are far apart interiorly"[31]. The action of the Holy Spirit is absolutely indispensable if this communion between the brethren is to be created. It will be seen in mutual charity. But charity which prepares us for the contemplation of the Father is rooted in the imitation of Jesus who humbled himself in order to show man his true condition and lead him to his true destiny. In fact such humility is basic to all community life. Blessed Guerric, the great Cistercian father of the second generation, noted that "it is the glory of charity to abase oneself before one's friends"[32].

To be at each other's service and dependent on one another calls for a reversal of our usual egocentric attitudes. It is no longer I but my brother who must be served first. As St Benedict says, "they should try to be the first to show respect, each to the other" (RB 72:4). This desire is not innate in us. The common life provides an excellent place for us to learn to respect each other, for it is the place where contrary aspirations and conflicting interests inevitably come up against each other.

After a sort of honeymoon within the community the faults and limitations of the brethren begin to appear, and to contrast strongly with the ideal community we have envisaged. They will appear as an obstacle on the spiritual path until we accept the truth about ourselves. If we are to form a real bond with others, we must know ourselves and our limitations and faults. We are no better than others. We too need mercy and if the truth be known we need it more than others. We must learn to know the tender mercy of God which pursues us even when we sin. God's love is forgiveness. And we too are called on to show each other the same forgiving love.

When we have experienced God's tenderness we will be able to share it with our brothers. Every Christian community is essentially built on mutual pardon. Without doubt this is the reason why St Benedict wanted every fault and failing, however slight, to be confessed to the abbot and the community (RB 41:3). The humility of the confession will bring the pardon of all and increase mutual love. Even the penance which St Benedict enjoins, perhaps too generously by our modern standards, had no other aim but to re-introduce the erring brother into the communion of love.

This fraternal support by confession and forgiveness still holds today. The way it is brought about has changed. A small group gets together voluntarily, where each accepts that he is open to the fraternal admonition of the others, while being concerned in his turn about their spiritual welfare and progress. St Benedict instructs the brethren to listen to and obey each other (RB 72:6), because each one ministers the word of life to the others, in the Holy Spirit. Fraternal correction is a powerful means of nourishing that spirit and creating a deep-seated cohesion within a community. Whenever a monk admits to the others that he has done something to impede the progress of the community, his confession supports the group and encourages each individual to greater responsibility. The same holds if he becomes aware of this through the frankness of his brothers. Thus is forged the one heart and the one mind of the community of which the Acts of the Apostles speaks in describing the first Christian community in Jerusalem, itself the prototype of every cenobitic community. Commenting on this, St Bernard says:

> Let there be therefore, brethren, a unity of spirit; let hearts be united in loving, seeking and clinging to the same object; and in everyone esteeming each other in the same way. And thus external divisions will be neither a danger nor a scandal. Each one can have his own way of dealing with situations, each his own view of the world's affairs, and each one his different gift of grace. Neither will all have to engage in the same activity. But interior unity and unanimity will unify this multiplicity, and the cement of charity and the bond of peace will hold it together.[33]

127

## 5. *Spiritual friendship*

Friendship is an excellent way of learning to love. The word occurs only rarely in the ancient monastic writers, apart from John Cassian who is a notable exception.[34] But with the Cistercians of the twelfth century both the word and the reality suddenly and strikingly appear. We cannot doubt that friendship was widely cultivated in the Cistercian cloisters. The masters of the spiritual life sang of its delights and celebrated its spiritual qualities, and this despite their warnings against its pitfalls and dangers. To their eyes it appeared as a place of meeting with the Lord, to which he would sometimes come to give the grace of love to a heart he had already drawn to himself.

Paraphrasing the well-known saying of St John, the great English Cistercian Aelred of Rievaulx dared to write: "God is friendship and he who lives in friendship lives in God and God lives in him" (cf 1 Jn 4:16). Aelred knew how a friend becomes the sacrament which reveals the love of Jesus. A simple glance can awaken a heart, and inspire it to go out of itself to give itself to another. Friendship has the effect of putting two persons into communion with each other so that their hearts grow and open to love and to prayer at the same moment. Unlikely as it may sound, it is often true. Any stirring of love restores some integrity to the being of the one who loves, enabling him to grow. By means of friendship prayer can be enkindled and burn in the heart. Has not all true friendship the mission of making one's friendship with Jesus, perhaps until now felt only vaguely, something central to one's life?

Aelred describes at length the marvellous process of grace whereby friendship between brothers leads into friendship with Jesus, makes it grow, deepens it, renders it solid and at the same time jealous —like any great love. Friendship with Jesus is the aim of all fraternal life. When this comes into the presence of Jesus, it becomes outwardly more discreet. But in fact through this very reserve, it deepens and grows in God.

Friendship with Jesus like all other friendship feels the need to allow the friend to enter deeply into one's heart, so that he can possess it entirely. It calls forth reserve, silence, intimacy, interiority. All monastic solitude is at the service of such friendship. The silence of the cloister helps Cistercians cultivate this presence of Jesus so that he can become their intimate companion in solitude. Isolation is no longer possible, but only intimacy between two persons, which draws strength from the life they share.

## 6. *Everyone has his own gift from God* (RB 40:1)

Friendship presupposes both equality and complementarity. It feeds on this diversity which enables each of the friends to give something to the other. Likewise in the common life this exchange of different charisms can nourish mutual love. There are, however, many differences between people—the character of each, his experience before he came to the monastery. The monks come from different backgrounds. Perhaps one was a student, another a worker, another in the army. One may be from the city, another from the countryside. At the time of St Benedict there were free men and slaves. What matters is that the monastery be truly ecumenical; it does not obliterate differences but leads them to convergence in Christ. In this connection St Benedict reminds us that we all serve the same master and the one Lord (RB 61:10). In fact these differences provide grounds for sharing and for mutual respect, which cannot but be for the strengthening of the community.

As well as these natural differences between the brethren, there is also a difference in grace. All indeed are Cistercians, but the Cistercian charism contains many nuances. Every community should try to harmonise these differences and accommodate the nuances of grace by allowing for a pluralism of vocation which is not destructive of unity. This will be done if the pluralism is the fruit of a liberty by which the Holy Spirit leads each one. Many and diverse riches come together to form the unity of the Cistercian church.

Cistercian writers in the twelfth century loved to compare the monastery to the little house in Bethany which Jesus loved to visit to be with his friends. Certainly Jesus must be the soul and centre of the monastery. But our fathers also saw the three friends of Bethany—Martha, Mary and Lazarus—as three types of people, all of whom are found in the monastery.

Lazarus they saw as the beginner who is still busy weeping for his sins and amending his life. Martha symbolised the officials of the monastery who are preoccupied with the cares of serving their brethren. Mary stood for those brethren who can more freely enjoy leisure for *lectio* and prayer. This description presupposes that in the same monastery we have occupations and perhaps timetables which are somewhat varied. The important thing is that each one cultivate the grace he has been given without looking askance at that of his brother. He will do this if he opts once and for all for the part of Mary, throwing all as she did at the feet of Christ, and abandoning everything for the word Christ is offering her. "O Blessed house", says St Bernard, "where Martha complains of Mary".[35]

The abbot must discern the particular grace of each one, which can change from one moment to another. At one time, God may call a man to the desert to allow him to taste his intimacy. At other times the same monk may be called to a more demanding service of his brethren. It is still God who calls him and he does not abandon him in his work, no matter how it draws him out of himself. This diversity of function is needed if all graces are to be present in one community and be shared in by everyone. The grace of one becomes the grace of all. The hermit who lives alone must be content with a grace that is strictly his own, but the cenobite who lives with others possesses all that they receive. How can he complain about having received but little? How can he envy the gifts of others when everything belongs to all? St Bernard says:

> It is a glorious thing for men to dwell together in one house with one mind. How good and how pleasant to see brothers living in unity! You can see one lamenting his sins, another praising God; this one ministering to all, another teaching and instructing; this one praying, that one reading. One confesses his sins, another does penance for his. One shines for his charity, another for his humility. One can be seen to be humble in prosperity, another patient in adversity. This one is engaged in work, another rests in contemplation. Thus we can say: Truly this is the camp of God; this is an awesome place (Gen. 32:2 and 28:17). It is none other than the house of God and gate of heaven! What then, faithful soul, should you look for in all this? Gather together all the virtues which abound in the house of

God, and make them a treasure. Let them teach you how to live. And you who formerly dwelt in the region of the shadow of death, pass now to the region of life and truth.[36]

## 7. *Dialogue between brothers*

One of the essential words in the monastic vocabulary and also one of the oldest is the Latin word *"collatio"*, which means essentially a conversation. However, a *collatio* is neither recreation nor mere passing the time but a serious mutual interchange in which each one benefits the other. We have already seen that the abbot is called on frequently—indeed in ideal conditions he is called on daily—to share his spiritual experience with his brethren. But the monks also have a word to say to each other.

When there is a decision to be made concerning the community, St Benedict orders the abbot to assemble the brethren and listen attentively to what each one has to say on the subject. He tells him that he is to listen especially to the youngest, for he seems to have known by experience that it is often to the young that God reveals his will (RB 3:3). The Holy Spirit is at work in the community and the abbot must listen carefully, even though the final responsibility is his. Today we have many ways of ensuring this responsible participation in the life of the community. Since the Vatican Council it has developed in ways that before were quite unknown in monastic history.

The most important decisions, canonical visitations and even general chapters are prepared for by the whole community. Commissions to deal with economic, liturgical or pastoral problems are elected by the monks. The brethren exchange ideas in small groups, and then in the presence of the community they look at the whole picture and arrive at their decisions. If the abbot so directs, a secret vote may decide the issue. It is by no means essential that a democratic majority decide the matter. Sometimes it is not even necessary that the majority express its view for the abbot to sense what is the right thing to do. What is important is that by listening to each other we gradually discern the will of God. This does not necessarily correspond with either the ideas of the abbot or the decision of the majority. It is found rather in an agreement in the community, what we nowadays call consensus, or what St Bernard called "the common will". This emerges when the abbot and the monks truly listen to each other, each one being prepared to renounce his own viewpoint. The abbot's charism, which belongs to his office, is not to impose his own viewpoint, but to discern, perhaps sooner than others, how the community consensus is emerging and what direction it is taking.

In this way, the abbot is the bond of unity and of love in the community even at the moment of decision. And in this way too, the decision, which in the mind of St Benedict is always the ultimate responsibility of the abbot, will reflect the will of God for the community more surely. While this may be painful for some, it will nonetheless be a source of communion and peace.

These meetings of the brethren are not concerned only or even chiefly with community government. In any community today you will find groups of about five to eight monks who meet weekly or perhaps less often. They come together to exchange ideas on a spiritual topic, to discuss the gospel, to prepare the Sunday liturgy, to pray together, or maybe for a mutual avowal of faults and problems. Most of the time these groups are set up spontaneously and attract people with some spiritual affinity. The fraternal support which a monk can find in them can play a decisive role at a time of temptation.

## 8. *The paradise of the cloister*

The writers of the Middle Ages did not hesitate to compare the cloister to paradise. They had in mind both the earthly and the heavenly paradise. They saw the monk as having rediscovered the first, when God comes again to take the evening air and share intimacy with his friends. And they considered too that the monk had already in some way entered the heavenly paradise in that even here below he was tasting its joys. While the image is beautiful we must admit that the road ahead of the monk is long and arduous. We must also stress that the community life is not something which is merely of service to one's personal vocation to solitude. In the path of the Gospel, fraternal community life is its own end. It is a fulness of love and presupposes an exceptional degree of mutual forgiveness. If we seek to live in friendship with Jesus and the brethren with one heart and one mind, we are really living the very life of the Church of Jesus, and seeking to live the life here which Jesus has promised us, in him, by his Spirit, in the presence of the Father.

The following passage from the *Rule of St Benedict* makes this clear. The saint here sketches a portrait of the ideal community life that he proposes to his monks. Normally St Benedict's language is sober and matter-of-fact, but here his pen trembles with an emotion which shines out through the words of this outstanding passage of the rule for monks:

> Just as there is a wicked zeal of bitterness which separates from God and leads to hell, so there is a good zeal which separates from evil and leads to God and everlasting life. This, then, is the good zeal which monks must foster with fervent love: they should try to be the first to show respect for each other (Rom. 12:10), supporting with the greatest patience one another's weaknesses of body or behaviour, and earnestly competing in obedience to one another. No one is to pursue what he judges better for himself, but instead what he judges better for someone else. To their fellow monks they should show the pure love of brothers, to God loving fear, to their abbot unfeigned and humble love. Let them prefer nothing whatever to Christ, and may he bring us all together to everlasting life.[37]

133

# Chapter 10

## WITH MARY, THE MOTHER OF JESUS

There is one important aspect of Cistercian spirituality about which we have not yet spoken. That is the place held by the Blessed Virgin Mary. The Order placed itself under her patronage from its beginning, and dedicated all its churches to her. The Cistercian writers of the twelfth century sang of the Holy Mother of God with a filial piety matched only by the theological exactitude of their language. St Bernard, supreme among all the others, merited the title "Lutanist of Mary".

This devotion to the Blessed Virgin is more than the fruit of the marian movement in the Church at one period in its history. In the mystery of the Virgin Mary, Cistercian monks have recognised certain traits peculiar to their way of life. From the beginning they have felt drawn to her as to a source of life and example. One of the major texts of the General Chapter on Renewal says: "We pursue this search (for God) under a rule and an abbot, in a community of charity, in which all are equally responsible and to which we are committed by stability. The community lives in a climate of silence and separation from the world which favours and expresses this opening to God in contemplation after the example of Mary who kept all these things and meditated on them in her heart"[38]. When we try to speak of the role of Cistercian monks in the Church the image of the Virgin Mary comes irresistibly to mind.

### 1. "According to your Word"

Mary was so receptive to the Word of God that she conceived him in her womb and gave him birth here in our midst. We have seen the importance for the monk of listening to this word and welcoming it. This welcome is the key to his existence. There he finds the secret energy which gives him strength to continue on his way.

"Man cannot live on bread alone; he lives on every word that God utters" (Mt. 4:4). During the long moments of *lectio divina*, during the hours of the divine office, the word of God is the principal nourishment of the monk.

He listens to this word in the Church and for the Church. God never ceases to speak his word of love, and he desires that some among us would give him their ear and their heart. Not only will they find their joy and their peace in that word but they will be transformed by it. The word of God is always a creative word. It does not return to God without having carried out his will (cf Is. 55:11).

In the Virgin Mary the word brought about the Incarnation of the Word. In the Church today it continually bears fruit anew. It brings to birth, it makes holy, it bears witness. And when we speak of the Church we mean especially the hearts of believers who are truly given up to the word of God. By his vocation the monk is one of these. He is, as it were, one of the entry-points where the word can come into this world.

## 2. *A heart pregnant with the Word*

"A heart pregnant with the Word" is the expression applied by Blessed Guerric to the Virgin Mary and to the monk. He sees the monk as conceiving the Word in his heart by prolonged contact with the word[39]. For nine months the Word of God slowly matured in the womb of the Virgin Mary. Down the years and the centuries, the word has continued to grow in the heart of the world. It is ceaselessly sown by the Church in the heart of everyone who listens and puts their hope of eternal life in it. The monk in his turn bears the life of God even more deeply in his heart. It matures slowly in order to become incarnate in him. He has no other *raison d'être* than this.

As God once leaned down with infinite tenderness to the Virgin Mary, so today he leans down with the same love to those hearts in which the word is on the point of bearing fruit. These are the hearts in which the word is sown and grows. They act as a sort of matrix for the heart of the world which is already striving towards that new creation, the new world born of the Spirit and the Word. Those hearts are filled with the desire of God and even now his infinite love waits patiently for them.

Thus the word which the monk receives is not destined just for himself. Not that he must necessarily speak it to others. If the word remains deep in his own heart, it is so that taking root there it will give rise to new life. And that new life is the beginning of the new world which will be reborn when the figure of this world will have passed away. This is a mysterious reality. It is invisible to us, for it is of another order to that with which we deal every day. But for those who believe, it is already present in the Church and in the world. It prepares for and even inaugurates the time which is to come. It brings to birth the longing of the universe for the transfiguration of all things in the Spirit and in glory. The monk lovingly recollects himself around this seed, this spark of the life of God, and in doing this he carries the world to come in the very depths of his heart. The seed does not come from him. It is born of God. Like the Virgin Mary, the monk makes his heart and his body ready for it. He is entirely given up to waiting and listening. He looks forward to it in hope, knowing that his vocation is to nurture the seed of life.

This life of God does not belong to him. It is entrusted to him for others, for the centuries which are to come. And as a mother watches over the fruit she carries in her womb near her heart, so the monk nurtures the word in his heart. Little by little, the life of God takes possession of him. Expressed in him inwardly by God it seeks to express itself outwardly, in his body, in his psyche, in his every attitude. This work is not done without pain. It hurts in his very depths and even lacerates his body. The rebirth in the Spirit cannot take place without the pain of childbirth, without a strange mixture of suffering and of joy. The woman who is about to bear a child, said Jesus, suffers in her body, but is already full of joy because of the life which is about to be born, and which she can greet a few instants later. That life which is coming to birth in her makes her suffer, but it is also the cause of her joy — that this new being should come into the world (cf Jn 16:21). There is no better image for explaining what we have called the asceticism or discipline of the monastic life. Sometimes there is suffering caused by the weight of the new life which presses heavily upon us as we struggle towards the perfection to which we are called. It is the pain, if pain it be, of the bud which opens under the pressure of the life it contains.

## 3. *The prophetic word*

"Let it be done to me according to your word" (Lk. 1:38)*. When the Virgin Mary uttered these words, she gave herself up completely to the creative power of the word of God. In that power she conceived the Word in her womb, and brought him forth as her Son. She also received the power to proclaim the word in a new and up to then unknown way. She did this in her *Magnificat* and so she became a prophet.

Almost all the words of the *Magnificat* are taken from the Old Testament. They are the words of the prophets and of the psalms. The originality of the *Magnificat* lies not in the words but in the meaning with which these words are now clothed. They speak now not just of any intervention of God, but of his decisive coming to us in his Son. In the Song of Mary, the ancient biblical words acquired their definitive meaning. Henceforth they speak of Jesus Christ, whom God has sent, the Word Incarnate. Mary belongs to both the Old and the New Testaments, and as such she is a prophet. She shows a sensitivity and announces a new meaning which belong to the new age—that age which the Spirit has come to inaugurate in her person.

The words which the monk receives in order to share them with others have this same quality. He too lives on the frontier between two epochs in the history of salvation. Not that he stands between the Old Testament and the New, but between the time of the Church and that of the world to come. He is rooted in the former, and already has a foretaste and even almost a vision of the latter in his heart. When St Bernard speaks of the experience of things to come, an experience which the monk sometimes receives, he

* Not the NEB, as the author's meaning requires that the word "word" be used.

uses the word "*interim*". The monk belongs to the time in between. Like the Virgin Mary, he is an intermediary figure, standing on the threshold between time and eternity. He is both passing by and waiting.

The old world is still there and the monk belongs to it. But the new world has begun to break through, at least momentarily and in brief flashes. Without understanding it clearly the monk has received a sort of illumination of it. On his lips, as on those of the Virgin Mary, the words of the psalms have a new taste, the taste of the world to come.

In this sense the monk too is a prophet. His life is a prophetic sign at the heart of the world. Not for him to foretell future events which are already present to the Lord Jesus in glory, but the Holy Spirit does give him a sensitivity which enables him know the direction of events and the meaning of trials. This is not merely emotional, a pious feeling or instinct. The life of the monk is an image of what we await in eternal life.

The monastery with its bell tower visible in the early morning light, or outlined against the clouds, is a mysterious call for those who can hear it. It is more than just a call, it is a magnetic pole. Many, believers and unbelievers alike, are intrigued by it, for it speaks to them of something beyond itself. They come to the cloister either to stay a while to share the life of the monks in the guest house or at least to pause a moment in the church during the divine office. This is the essential word that every monastic community is called on to say to those who pass by—the brotherhood of believers at prayer, radiating a peace and joy so rare in our world today. A simple word but an insistent and powerful one, it speaks not only to believers but to those also who know nothing more of the monastic life beyond the fact that it exists. Some monks may be called on to say more than this. They do not go out of their solitude to preach the word. People come to them. Sometimes perhaps they come in greater numbers than the monk might wish for. They are looking for a word of discernment which will be the beginning of salvation for them. They seek a word of prophecy which will tell them the meaning of trials and events, which will show them the road along which God comes to meet his people. In the shade of every

monastery there is this ministry of spiritual companionship for those
who seek it.

## 5. *Spouse of the Word*

In the church of St Benedict's monastery at Subiaco is a beautiful
fourteenth century fresco depicting the Assumption of our Lady
into heaven. This is no majestic Byzantine virgin, no hieratic figure
garbed in profound recollection, her eyes straining towards the
invisible, but a more gracious and affable lady. She is seated beside
Christ on a single throne, and his right arm encircles her shoulder.
Her hand rests on his shoulder and he draws her imperceptibly
towards himself. Her head inclines gently to him, and the scene
is surrounded by rejoicing angels. Done by an unknown Siennese
artist, this is one of the most touching and tender portrayals of the
mystery of the Assumption ever painted.

It was under the invocation of this mystery that the order
dedicated all its churches to the Blessed Virgin, and it was the
favourite theme of the great Cistercian writers who sang of her.
In the Virgin Mary the love of God for his creatures reaches its
apogee and fulfilment—the fulness of beauty and of love. The Virgin
Mary is the fulness of all beauty and of love. She alone is already
the plenitude of the Church. She is the Bride of the Word and his
eternal joy. She is the joy of God, who through her has assumed
all humanity into the Incarnate Word, come to inaugurate the new
temple, in the heart of the Trinity, where praise and thanksgiving
will be forever sung. This heavenly liturgy is even now shared in
by the liturgical assembly of the Church. In every liturgy "a door
is opened in heaven" (Rev. 4:1), which enables us to see some
reflection of the beauty and love which are in God. The monk is
present to this every day and every night. The door is open not
only in the community of his brethren gathered for worship but
also in his own heart. We have already quoted the saying of Isaac
the Syrian: "Enter into your own heart and find the door that opens
on Paradise"[40].

In the deepest centre of his own being, the monk finds the
marriage chamber where the Spouse awaits, towards which the

whole world is hastening throughout all time, as towards a joy and beauty without end. It is there that the voice of the Spirit resounds, and to that voice are joined those of the Spouse and the monk, crying out: "Come, Lord Jesus" (Rev. 22:20).

God has no greater joy than that the sinner should return to him (Lk. 15:7). It is in knocking at the door of his own heart that he will come to the door leading to God. God wills that the prostitute, who is washed in the blood of the Lamb, should precede all others into the kingdom (Mt. 21:31), and that the good thief who looked at Jesus would that day enter paradise (Lk. 23:43). The monk *is* these sinners. It is in his very sinfulness and weakness that God will work his wonders and show his mighty power. The monk has received everything from God, even that beauty which increases in him daily and gradually transforms him into the likeness of Christ. Over the long years of monastic life he has grown old. Yet he remains ever young, with unquenchable hope and with wonder at the goodness and kindness of God. His eyes are the eyes of a child who never ceases to marvel at the mighty deeds of God.

This beauty is the beauty of the Church. It comes to the face of a man or a woman from within. It is like the glow of a fire that is just below the surface. It is also the beauty of the Spirit. It is a reflection of the glory of God which shines in the face of Jesus Christ (cf 2 Cor 4:6) and in the faces of all who walk by his light.

The Greeks have a word for the monk—they call him "*kalogiros*". It means a good and beautiful old man. The Latin tradition calls him a man of God. Is there any achievement greater or more splendid than this, that a man, humble and unaware, should reflect the goodness and the beauty of God?

# References

1. "Decree on the Renewal of Religious Life", 2(a), in *Vatican Council II: Conciliar and post-Conciliar Documents,* ed. A. Flannery (Dublin and Wilmington), p. 621.

2. "Little Exordium of Cîteaux", tr. B. Lackner, in L. Lekai, *The Cistercians* (Kent State, 1977), p. 460.

3. *ibid.* p. 460.

4. *ibid.*

5. *ibid.* p. 461.

6. *ibid.*

7. *ibid.* p. 444.

8. "Message of Contemplative Monks to the Synod of Bishops at Rome, 1967". This message was the work of Dom André Louf, Thomas Merton and Dom J.-B. Porion, Procurator General of the Carthusians. It is published in English in *Cistercian Studies* vol. 2, 1967, pp. 269-73.

9. I. Hausherr, SJ. *Les lecons d'un contemplatif: Le traité de l'oraison d'Evagre le Pontique* (Paris, 1960), p. 168. cf also: *Evagrius Ponticus: The Praktikos & the Chapters on Prayer,* tr. J.E. Bamberger, (Spencer, Mass., 1970), p. 76.

10. "Message of Contemplative Monks to the Synod of Bishops", *op. cit.,* p. 270.

11. St Bernard, "Sermons on the Song of Songs. Sermon 43:3", quoted from *The Works of St Bernard of Clairvaux,* vol. 3, p. 221, "On the Song of Songs, 2", tr. K. Walsh (Kalamazoo, Mich., 1976).

12. St Ignatius of Antioch, *Letter to the Romans* (From the Latin).

13. St Jerome, "Letters 22:17", tr. W.H. Fremantle in "St Jerome's Letters and Select Works" in *Library of Nicene and Post-Nicene Fathers* (Grand Rapids, Mich., 1954), vol. 6, p. 28.

14. "Letter of St Macarius to his sons", Latin text in Migne, *Patrologia Graeca* 34, 406. There is a French translation with bibliographical references in *Collectanea Cisterciensium Reformatorum XXIV* (1962), pp. 52-9 (the author seems to have made his own translation; passages quoted here are from the Latin with reference to Louf).

15. ibid.

16. Abbot Poemen, English text in *The Sayings of the Desert Fathers*, tr. Sr. B. Ward, SLG (Kalamazoo, Mich. and London, 1975), p. 146:54.

17. *Isaac the Syrian, Treatises, 66.* English tr. A.J. Wensinck (Wiesbaden, 1969), p. 315.

18. *ibid. 65*, p. 302.

19. Quoted in I. Gorainoff, *Seraphin de Sarov* (Begrolles-en-Mauges, 1973), p. 50.

20. *Isaac the Syrian, op. cit.*, 2, p. 8.

21. *"De Domo Interiori seu De Conscientia"*, in P. Dion, *Oeuvres Complètes de S. Bernard*, t. 1., (Paris, 1860), pp. 1-50.

22. *Guerric of Igny. Liturgical Sermons*, vol. 2., tr. the monks of Mount St Bernard Abbey (Spencer, Mass., 1971) (Cistercian Fathers Series, no. 32), p. 180.

23. Peter of Celle, "Letters", 176, in Migne, *Patrologia Latina* 202, 635.

24. *Guerric of Igny, op. cit.*, p. 184.

25. John Cassian, "Institutes, Bk. 2, Ch. 14", tr E.C. Gibson in *Library of Nicene and Post-Nicene Fathers* (Grand Rapids, Mich., 1973), vol. 11, p. 211.

26. William of St-Thierry "Vita Sancti Bernardi", 4:23, in Migne, PL 185, 240.

27. *ibid.*

28. St Bernard, *Letters, 76*, tr. B. Scott James (London, 1953), p. 107. (This is letter 73:2 (p. 180) in the critical edition by J. Leclercq and H. Rochais, *S. Bernardi Opera* vol. VII, Rome, 1974.)

29. William of St-Thierry, *op. cit.*, 7:35, in PL 185, 247-8.

30. Quoted by J. Leclercq in "Inedits Bernardins dans un manuscrit d'Orval", in *Analecta Monastica* 1 (Studia Anselmiana, 20, 1972), p. 176.

31. St Bernard, *Sentences III: 108*, in J. Leclercq and H. Rochais, *S Bernardi Opera*, vol. VI/2, (Rome, 1972), p. 176.

32. Guerric of Igny, "Sermon for Ascension", in *op. cit.*, p. 105.

33. St Bernard, "For Septuagesima 2", in *op. cit.*, vol. IV, p. 352.

34. John-Cassian, "Conferences XVI. First Conference of Abbot Joseph on Friendship", in *op. cit.*, p. 451.

35. St Bernard, "Sermon for the Assumption, 3, 2", in *op. cit.*, vol. VI/1, p. 239.

36. St Bernard, "*Sermon de Diversis* 42, 2", in *op. cit.*, vol. VI/1, p. 258.

37. *Rule of St Benedict ch. 72*, ed Timothy Fry (Collegeville, 1981), p. 293.

38. "Declaration on the Cistercian Life", General Chapter, OCSO, 1969. *See Appendix A below.*

39. Guerric of Igny, "Sermon on the Annunciation, 2, 4-5", in *op. cit.* p. 44.

40. Isaac the Syrian, *op. cit.* 2., p. 8.

*Appendix A: Basic Texts*

1. *Cistercian Beginnings*

EXORDIUM CISTERCII

1. *Departure of the Cistercian Monks from Molesme*
In the diocese of Langres there lay, as is well known, a monastery
by the name of Molesme; it was of great renown and outstanding in
religious fervour. Within a short time of its foundation God in his
goodness enriched it with the gift of his graces, raised it to honour
with the presence of distinguished men, and caused it to be as great
in possessions as it was resplendent in virtues. But, because possessions and virtues are not usually steady companions, several
members of that holy community, men truly wise and filled with
higher aspirations, decided to pursue heavenly studies rather than to
be entangled in earthly affairs. Accordingly, these lovers of virtue
soon came to think about that poverty which is fruitful to man.
They realized that, although life in that place was a godly and
upright life, they observed the Rule they had vowed to keep in a
way short of their desire and intention. They spoke amongst themselves and asked one another how they were to fulfill the verse:
"I will fulfill my vows to you, vows which I made with my own
lips" (Ps 64:13). What more needs to be said? After common
deliberation, together with the father of that monastery, Robert of
blessed memory, twenty-one monks went out to try to carry out
jointly what they had conceived with one spirit. Eventually, after
many labours and extreme difficulties, which all who wish to devote
their life to Christ must endure, they reached their goal. They came
to Cîteaux, which was then a place of horror, a vast wilderness.
Realizing that the asperity of the place accorded well with the strict
design they had already conceived (in their minds), the soldiers of
Christ found the place, almost as though divinely prepared, to be as
alluring as their design had been dear.

2. *Beginnings of the Monastery of Cîteaux*
Thus in the year 1098 of the Incarnation of Our Lord, supported
with the counsel and strengthened with the authority of the

147

venerable Hugh, archbishop of the church of Lyons, and at the time legate of the Apostolic See, and of the God-fearing man, Walter, bishop of Chalons, and of Odo, the illustrious duke of Burgundy, these men began to transform the solitude they had found into an abbey; abbot Robert received the care of the monks and the shepherd's staff from the bishop of the diocese; and under him the others vowed stability in the place. But, after a short time it happened that the same abbot Robert was reclaimed by the monks of Molesme, and was returned to Molesme on the order of Pope Urban II and with the permission and consent of Walter, bishop of Chalons. He was replaced by Alberic, a religious and holy man. For the sake of peace this wise agreement was made between the monasteries and confirmed by the pope: henceforth neither of them would (permanently) accept the other's monk without a proper recommendation. Through the solicitude and industry of its new father and with God's generous assistance, the New Monastery thereafter advanced in holiness, excelled in fame, and witnessed the increase of its temporal goods. The man of God, Alberic, who successfully ran his race for nine years (Ph. 2:16), obtained the crown of eternity in the tenth year. He was succeeded by the lord Stephen, an Englishman by nationality, an ardent lover of and staunch champion of religious life, poverty and regular discipline. In his days, the words of Scripture came true: "The eyes of the Lord are upon the just and his ears hear their prayers" (Ps. 33:16). The little flock voiced its one and only complaint: that it was small in numbers. As I said, the "poor of Christ" came to fear and to dread almost to the point of despair one thing alone: that they might not be able to leave behind heirs to their poverty. For their neighbours applauded their holy life but abhorred its austerity and thus kept from imitating the men whose fervour they approved. Yet God, who can easily make great things from small ones and many things from a few, beyond all expectation, so aroused the hearts of many to the imitation of these monks that in the cell where the novices are tested, thirty had come to live under the same discipline: clerics as well as laymen, even nobles and men of power in the eyes of the world. Upon this so sudden and happy heavenly visitation the barren one which had no offspring began, not without reason, to rejoice: "Once forsaken, she now came to have many sons" (Is. 54:1). And God did not cease to multiply His people, and to increase their joy, so that within about twelve years the happy mother came to see twenty abbots, drawn from her own sons as well as from the sons of her sons, like olive branches around her table.

Indeed she did not think it out of order to follow the example of the holy Father Benedict whose Rule she embraced. Hence, as soon as the new plantation began to produce offshoots, blessed Father Stephen in his watchful wisdom provided a document of admirable discretion; it served as a trimming knife which was to cut off the outgrowth of division which, if unchecked, could suffocate the fruit of mutual peace. Very appropriately, he wished the document to be called a Charter of Charity, for, clearly, its whole content so breathed love that almost nothing else is seen to be treated there than this: "Owe no man anything, but to love one another" (Rom 13:8).

> *Translated from the Latin by Bede K. Lackner, O.Cist., in Louis J. Lekai,* The Cistercians. Ideals and Reality *(Kent, Ohio: Kent State University Press, 1977).*

## 2. *Cistercian Life Today*

A DECLARATION ON CISTERCIAN LIFE BY THE 1969 GENERAL CHAPTER of the Order of Cistercians of the Strict Observance

We Cistercian Monks feel a deep desire to interpret for our own times the traditions which our Fathers have handed down to us. Yet we must admit that we are faced with a variety of differing trends in our Order which characterize its present situation. We may feel at times that certain of these trends could well obstruct the renewal and healthy evolution of the Order.

And yet, when these difficulties came to light at the opening of this Chapter for renewal we all discovered a profound sense of communion in the lived experience of our common spiritual values. We are convinced that the work of this Chapter will become constructive to the degree that we foster this communion and the mutual confidence which it inspires.

We shall do this by recognizing all that really unites us in the Holy Spirit, rather than by trying to impose unity through a legislation that would determine observances down to the last detail. Individual communities can in fact look after such details according to local needs and in conformity with the directives of the General Chapter—so long as our wholly contemplative orientation is maintained. We are convinced that the best laws are those which follow and interpret life, and it is in the concrete experience of our

149

Cistercian vocation that we would first of all recognize this life.

Our wish is to clarify the content of this experience which we all share and by so doing to further as best we can the values which inspire it. That is why we feel moved to make the following Declaration on our own particular way of life:

Following the first Fathers of our Order we find in the holy *Rule of St Benedict* the practical interpretation of the Gospel for ourselves. A sense of the Divine Transcendence and of the Lordship of Christ not only pervades the whole of this Rule but also permeates our life, totally orientated towards an experience of the Living God.

God calls and we respond by truly seeking Him as we follow Christ in humility and obedience. With hearts cleansed by the Word of God, by vigils, by fasting and by an unceasing conversion of life, we aim to become ever more disposed to receive from the Holy Spirit the gift of pure and continual prayer.

This search for God is the soul of our monastic day, a day composed of the *Opus Dei, Lectio divina* and manual work. Our Cistercian life is basically simple and austere. It is truly poor and penitential "in the joy of the Holy Spirit". Through the warmth of their welcome and hospitality our communities share the fruit of their contemplation and their work with others.

We carry out this search for God under a Rule and an Abbot in a community of love where all are responsible. It is through stability that we commit ourselves to this community. It lives in an atmosphere of silence and separation from the world, and fosters and expresses its openness to God in contemplation . . . treasuring, as Mary did, "all these things, pondering them in her heart".

The Church has entrusted a mission to us which we wish to fulfill by the response of our whole life . . . "To give clear witness to that heavenly home for which every man longs, and to keep alive in the heart of the human family the desire for this home . . . as we bear witness to the majesty and love of God and to the brotherhood of all men in Christ."

# 3. STATUTE ON UNITY AND PLURALISM
## of the 1969 General Chapter O.C.S.O.

## *Guidelines and Conditions for Applying Them*

This present General Chapter is convinced that "the unity which is based on charity and which has been the strength and beauty of the Cistercian Order ever since its origin "(Letter, PAUL VI to Abbot General), will best be served today by a deep sense of communion in the lived experience of our common spiritual values. That is why the present Chapter, in its Declaration on the Cistercian Life, has already insisted on the contemplative orientation and fundamental observances of our Order.

In the present Statute those observances which demand special attention in our times are presented in a more concrete fashion. Thus the fundamental values of our life are guaranteed without imposing a detailed uniformity, where in fact a legitimate diversity should exist. Conditions are laid down so that each community, in union with the other monasteries of the Order and following these guidelines, may deepen its own living experience of the Cistercian life.

GUIDELINES:

1. Faithful to the thought of their Founders, Cistercian monks live under a Rule and an Abbot. They live, united in the love of Christ, in a community which is stable and effectively separated from the world.

2. The Abbot, as spiritual father of his community, should try to discover the will of God. One important way of doing this is by listening to his brethren in the spirit of Chapter 3 of the Rule.

3. In our daily horarium we keep the balance between the *Opus Dei, Lectio divina* and manual work, as required by the Rule of St Benedict.

4. The hour of rising is so regulated that Vigils, which follows it, should keep its traditional character of nocturnal prayer—as we watch for the coming of the Lord.

5. The monk, who is tending to a life of continual prayer, needs a fixed amount of prayer each day. The Abbot will see to this for the community as a whole and for each individual monk in particular.

151

6. This search for a life of prayer should be lived in an atmosphere of recollection and silence for which all are responsible. In particular, the great silence at night and the silence in the regular places will be maintained.

7. Separation from the world demands that journeys out of the monastery should be infrequent and only for serious reasons. The use of radio and television will be exceptional. Discretion is needed in the use of other media of communication.

8. Our monasteries should practice generous hospitality, but this should not be allowed to interfere with the contemplative nature of our way of life.

9. Our diet should be simple and frugal. The monastic practice of fasting and abstinence should be retained.

10. The habit should be retained as the distinctive sign of our Order. Its use can differ from house to house.

11. The life of the community, as of each monk, should be marked by simplicity and poverty. Fraternal corrections in the spirit of the Gospel is a help in this direction.

CONDITIONS:

12. Within the limits of the above guidelines the monasteries of our Order are free to arrange the details of their observances. An effective consultation of the community should accompany these experiments— though the manner of it may vary.

13. Anything in the second or third parts of the Constitutions, or in the Usages, which does not fall under common law, retains only a directive force.

14. The results of these experiments will be reviewed by the Visitor, who will make a statement on them in his report to the General Chapter.

15. The experiments should be discussed at the Regional Conferences so that communities may be helped in their work of renewal.

*Appendix B*

## CISTERCIAN MONASTERIES TODAY

There are today some three hundred monasteries of monks and nuns following the Cistercian way. For historical reasons, they are divided into two 'Orders': the Order of Citeaux and the Order of Cistercians of the Strict Observance (sometimes called 'Trappists'). Visits may be arranged with the guestmaster/guestmistress of each house and additional information obtained on the life by writing to the vocation director.

The following monasteries are located in or near English-speaking areas.

■ *Order of Citeaux*          ♦ *Monks*
● *Strict Observance*         ♦ *Nuns*

### THE UNITED STATES AND CANADA

●♦ St Joseph's Abbey
   Spencer, Massachusetts 01562

●♦ Mount St Mary's Abbey
   Wrentham, Massachusetts 02093

■♦ Cistercian Monastery
   Mount Laurel Road
   Mount Laurel, New Jersey 08054

●♦ Genesee Abbey
   River Road
   Piffard, New York 14533

■♦ Monastery of St Mary
   Route 1
   New Ringgold, Pennsylvania
   17960

●♦ Holy Cross Abbey
   Route 2, Box 253
   Berryville, Virginia 22611

●♦ Our Lady of Mepkin Abbey
   Route 3, Box 800
   Moncks Corner, South Carolina
   29461

●♦ Holy Spirit Abbey
   2625 Highway 212 SW
   Conyers, Georgia 30208

●♦ Gethsemani Abbey
   Trappist, Kentucky 40073

●♦ New Melleray Abbey
   Dubuque, Iowa 52001

153

●◆ Our Lady of the
Mississippi Abbey
Dubuque, Iowa 52001

■◆ Our Lady of Springbank Abbey
34639 West Fairview Road
Oconomowoc, Wisconsin 53066

■◆ Valley of Our Lady Monastery
Route 1, Box 136
Prairie du Sac, Wisconsin 53578

●◆ Assumption Abbey
Route 5, Box 193
Ava, Missouri 65608

■◆ Our Lady of Dallas Abbey
Route 2, Box 1
Irving, Texas 75062

●◆ St Benedict's Monastery
Snowmass, Colorado 81654

●◆ Holy Trinity Abbey
Huntsville, Utah 84317

●◆ Santa Rita Abbey
Box 97
Sonoita, Arizona 85637

●◆ Redwoods Monastery
Whitehorn, California 95489

●◆ Abbey of New Clairvaux
P.O. Box 37
Vina, California 96092

●◆ Our Lady of Guadalupe Abbey
Box 97
Lafayette, Oregon 97127

●◆ Notre Dame du Calvaire
Route 3
Rogersville, New Brunswick
E0A 2T0

●◆ Notre-Dame de l'Assomption
de l'Acadie
Rogersville, Nouveau-Brunswick
E0A 2T0

●◆ Notre-Dame de Bon Conseil
Saint Romuald, c. Lévis, Québec
G6V 6V4

●◆ Notre-Dame du Lac
1600, St-Isidore, R.R.1
Oka, Québec
J0N 1E0

●◆ Notre-Dame de Mistassini
100 route des Trappistes
Mistassini, Québec
G0W 2C0

■◆ Notre Dame de Nazareth
C.P. 99
Rougemont, Québec
J0L 1M0

●◆ Cistercian Monastery of
Notre Dame
Route 5
Orangeville, Ontario
L9W 2Z2

●◆ Notre-Dame des Prairies/
Our Lady of the Prairies
Box 310
Holland, Manitoba
R0G 0X0

154

GREAT BRITAIN

●♦ Mount St Bernard Abbey
   Coalville, Leicester LE6 3UL
   (England)

●♦ Holy Cross Abbey
   276 Wimborne Road West
   Stapehill, Wimborne
   Dorset BH21 2EA
   (England)

●♦ Caldey Abbey
   Caldey Island, off Tenby
   Dyfed SA70 7UH
   (Wales)

●♦ Sancta Maria Abbey
   Nunraw, Haddington
   East Lothian EH41 4LW
   (Scotland)

*The following English houses belong to the Order of Bernardine Cistercian nuns:*

— Monastery of Our Lady of the Sacred Heart
   St Bernard's Convent
   Slough, Berks SL3 7AF

— Monastery of Our Lady of Good Counsel
   St Bernard's Convent
   Westcliff-on-Sea, Essex SS0 7JS

— Monastery of Our Lady of the Visitation
   St Bernard's Priory
   Hyning
   Warton, Carnforth, Lancs. LA5 9SE

*The following two houses belong to the Church of England:*

♦ Our Lady of West Malling Abbey
   Ewell Monastery
   West Malling, Kent ME19 6HH

♦ The House of Prayer
   Britwell Road
   Burnham, Bucks. SL1 8DQ

## IRELAND

●♦ Mount Melleray Abbey
  Cappoquin, Co. Waterford

●♦ Saint Mary's Abbey
  Glencairn, S.O., Co. Waterford

●♦ Mount St Joseph Abbey
  Roscrea, Co. Tipperary

●♦ Mellifont Abbey
  Collon, Co. Louth

●♦ Bolton Abbey
  Moone, Athy, Co. Kildare

●♦ Bethlehem Abbey
  11 Ballymena Road
  Portglenone, Ballymena,
  Co. Antrim
  (Northern Ireland) BT44 8BL

## OCEANIA

●♦ Southern Star Abbey
  Kopua, Takapau
  Hawkes Bay, New Zealand

●♦ Tarrawarra Abbey
  Yarra Glen, Victoria 3775
  Australia

## AFRICA

●♦ Our Lady of Victory Abbey
  P.O. Box 40
  Kipelion, Kenya

●♦ Our Lady of Praise
  Butende
  P.O. Box 660
  Masaka, Uganda

●♦ Cistercian Abbey
  P.O. Box 101
  Mankon–Bamenda,
  North West Province
  United Republic of Cameroon
  (West Africa)

●♦ Mount Calvary Monastery
  Awhum
  P.O. Box 698
  Enugu, Nigeria

●♦ Saint Justina Monastery
  P.O. Box 53
  Abakaliki, Anambra State
  Nigeria

■♦ Monastero dell'Assunta
  Casella post. 260
  Asmara, Ethiopia

■♦ Monastero Cisterciense
  Sub Post Office
  Mendida, per Debré Berhan
  Ethiopia

■♦ Cistercian Monastery
  P.O. Box 21902
  Addis Ababa
  Ethiopia

156

■♦ Residenza Cistercense
P.O. Box 61
Hosanna, Showa
Ethiopia

## ASIA

●♦ Torapisuto Shudoin
Oshima Tobetsu, Kamiiso
Hokkaido (049-02) Japan

●♦ Trappistines Shudoin (Tenshien)
Kamiyonokawa-cho Hokodate
Hokkaido (042) Japan

●♦ Monastere de Seiboen (Lourdes)
P.O. Box 83
Nishinomiya (662) Japan

●♦ Shito-kai, Imari no Seibo Shudoin
P.O. Box 3
Imari (848), Saga-ken, Japan

●♦ Torapisuto Shudoin
3101 Toyahara Nasu-Machi
Tochigi-ken (329-32) Japan

●♦ Miyako-jimi Shudoin
3979-3 Aza Karimata
Aza Marimata
Hirari-Shi
Okinawa-ken (906) Japan

●♦ Torapisuto Shudoin
Nishinodai Hiji
Oita-ken (879-15) Japan

●♦ Trappist Monastery
Lanto Island
P.O. Box 5, Peng Chau
Hong Kong

●♦ Pertapaan Rawaseneng
Temanggung (Jateng)
Indonesia

●♦ Our Lady of the Philippines
Jordan, Guimaras, Iloilo 5802
Philippine Islands

157

# CISTERCIAN PUBLICATIONS INC.

## Kalamazoo, Michigan

## TITLES LISTING

### THE CISTERCIAN FATHERS SERIES

## Texts and Studies
## in the
## Monastic Tradition

* Temporarily out of print                    † Forthcoming

# THE CISTERCIAN STUDIES SERIES

## MONASTIC TEXTS

## CHRISTIAN SPIRITUALITY

## MONASTIC STUDIES

## CISTERCIAN STUDIES

Saint Gregory Nazianzen: Selected Poems

Eight Chapters on Perfection and Angel's Song
(Walter Hilton)

Creative Suffering (Iulia de Beausobre)

Bringing Forth Christ. Five Feasts of the Child
Jesus (St Bonaventure)

Gentleness in St John of the Cross

*Distributed in North America only for Fairacres Press.*

### DISTRIBUTED BOOKS

St Benedict: Man with An Idea (Melbourne Studies)

The Spirit of Simplicity

Benedict's Disciples (David Hugh Farmer)

The Emperor's Monk: A Contemporary Life of
Benedict of Aniane

A Guide to Cistercian Scholarship (2nd ed.)

*North American customers may order
through booksellers or directly from
the publisher:*

Cistercian Publications
St Joseph's Abbey
Spencer, Massachusetts   01562
(508) 885–7011

Cistercian Publications
Editorial Offices
WMU Station
Kalamazoo, Michigan   49008
(616) 387–5090

*A complete catalogue of texts-in-
translation and studies on early,
medieval, and modern Christian
monasticism is available at no
cost from Cistercian Publications.*

*Cistercian monks and nuns have been
living lives of prayer & praise, meditation
& manual labor since the twelfth century.
They are part of an unbroken tradition
which extends back to the fourth century
and which continues today in the Catholic
church, the Orthodox churches, the
Anglican communion, and most recently,
in the Protestant churches.*

*Share their way of life and their search for
God by reading Cistercian Publications.*